# THE MODERN ROYAL NAVY

# THE MODERN ROYAL NAVY

A Guide to Britain's Sea Power

PAUL BEAVER

PATRICK STEPHENS

First published in 1988


British Library Cataloguing in Publication Data

Beaver, Paul
     The modern Royal Navy.
     1. Great Britain, Royal Navy.
     I. Title
     359'.00941          VA454

     ISBN 0-85059-924-5

Patrick Stephens Limited is part of the
Thorsons Publishing Group, Wellingborough,
Northamptonshire, NN8 2RQ, England

Printed in Great Britain by Woolnough
Bookbinding Limited, Irthlingborough,
Northamptonshire

10  9  8  7  6  5  4  3  2  1

# CONTENTS

# FOREWORD by Rear Admiral Robin Hogg, CB

Paul Beaver has met his difficult remit admirably in that this book sets out to be no more than a comprehensive introduction to the Royal Navy. He hints that the Navy may be facing cuts in its future share of the Defence Budget as though our dependence as a Nation on Maritime Power was in some way a sectarian issue between the Services in the Ministry of Defence. The truth is that most military operations of any consequence involve two or more Services. This is certainly true at sea where RAF aircraft are crucial to many operations. The Royal Navy too plays an increasingly important role in the Air Defence of our country, long held in the public imagination to be an exclusive responsibility of the RAF.

What of the future? Trident will most certainly ensure the credibility of our Independent National Strategic Nuclear Deterrent into the foreseeable future. I also see no sensible alternative for the Royal Navy to organic airpower at sea since no nation serious about being a maritime power can afford to be thwarted by the non-availability of airbases adjacent to the theatre of operations. The general purpose Destroyer or Frigate too is here to stay though it must change radically to keep pace with the threat and changes in the demographic structure of our country. Operations far from home, as in the Gulf today, demand the endurance and flexibility of such ships and their associated afloat support. Mines Counter-measures vessels will grow in importance and sophistication. Submarines, particularly those which are nuclear powered, remain the key to deep, covert penetration of and operations within enemy controlled waters.

Time does not stand still and the Royal Navy must capitalize on developments in science and technology. Nowhere are these factors more important than for the Surface Ship. We now have the capability to build ships of great hitting power, much increased resistance to damage and long endurance yet with a dramatically reduced ship's complement. Such ships are necessary now but will need to be supported by men organized, structured and supported quite differently from the sailor of today. Now is a time for men of vision in the Royal Navy, in industry and in politics to force through the necessary changes that will keep the Royal Navy, in Paul Beaver's words, 'the most professional in the world today'.

# INTRODUCTION and ACKNOWLEDGEMENTS

The modern Royal Navy is a highly professional organization which, although not the largest in the world, has a reputation for being the most professional. This was certainly proved in the spring of 1982 with the despatch of a Task Force to the South Atlantic and the resultant highly successful operation to liberate the Falkland and associated islands. To provide that manpower, equipment and expertise requires a highly complex and advanced technology-based force for sea, land and air operations.

To encapsulate completely the modern Royal Navy in a matter of 30,000 words is really an impossible task, but it is possible to give a general idea without making the contents too detailed and complex. The aim of this book is therefore to give a clear and concise introduction to the modern Royal Navy whether you are an enthusiast, a former member, a potential recruit or just interested in sailors and the sea.

The more serious student, and anyone interested in looking further into the modern Royal Navy, can consult several other books published by Patrick Stephens Limited including what has become a standard work, *The Encyclopaedia of the Modern Royal Navy* (including the Fleet Air Arm and the Royal Marines), and *The Encyclopaedia of the Fleet Air Arm since 1945*. In paperback, there is *Modern Royal Navy Warships*, *Modern Missile Systems* and *Today's Royal Marines* which will help to flesh out the bones of the modern Royal Navy.

To compile any book on the Royal Navy requires considerable co-operation. With this book, as with others in the past, I have been very lucky to have received full assistance. I would particularly like to thank Rear Admiral Guy Liardet CBE, formerly Director of Public Relations (Navy), and his successor, Captain Anthony Provest, Michael Hill (formerly public relations officer to CINCNAVHOME), Geoff Palmer (CINCFLEET PR) and the various commands and establishments including Commander C. S. C. Morgan (*Cambridge*), Lieutenant Commander Roger Warden (formerly *Invincible*), Lieutenant Commander D. J. Rees (FOF 3 staff), Lieutenant Commander Geoff Taylor (*Gannet*), Lieutenant Commander Cy Beattie (FONAC), First Officer

Wendy Ellison WRNR (CINCNAVHOME), Lieutenant Alistair McLaren (899 Squadron), Lieutenant R. M. Pendleton (*Sultan*), Second Officer Sue Elcomb WRNS (*Raleigh*), Second Officer Caroline Couzens WRNS (*Osprey*), Second Officer Tania Price WRNS (QARNNS/WRNS), Second Officer E. A. Pollitt WRNS (BRNC Dartmouth), Second Officer Heather Tuppen WRNS (Culdrose), Second Officer Emma Tortise WRNS (*Dolphin*), Sub Lieutenant John Lavery (*Drake*) and the Photographic Sections of various establishments. Robin Walker and Mike Lennon kindly helped with photographs.

*Paul Beaver*
*Old Basing, Hampshire*

# HISTORY SINCE 1945

The Second World War caused enormous changes in the Royal Navy, for not only was the force expanded to its largest ever size in terms of men, ships and aircraft, but also the attitudes of those who served changed out of all recognition. Then large numbers of 'hostilities only' officers and ratings were returned to civilian life, American lease-loaned aircraft and ships returned across the Atlantic and the Royal Navy returned to a peacetime existence. This of course meant contraction.

The war had also focused attention on new naval tactics and equipment. The use of atomic weapons against Japan had certainly shortened the war in the Pacific, but it also meant a new threat of radiation against which most if not all warships and shore establishments were ill-prepared. In addition, the naval aircraft, flying from 50,000-ton floating airfields and able to strike widely and with surprise, had led to a change in the hierarchy of naval operations. The aircraft carrier had proved itself in the Mediterranean Sea and the Indian and Pacific Oceans to be the capital ship of the future. The battleship, which had held the post without dispute since at least the time of the *Dreadnoughts* in 1901, had been seen to be vulnerable to air, surface and sub-surface action and would no longer dominate naval thinking.

The aircraft carrier demonstrated its ability to strike and therefore dominate the sea over the horizon, miles beyond the

*Last of the wartime destroyers,* Cavalier, *remained in commission until 1972 and is now preserved on Tyneside, where she was built.*

reach of even the largest battleship guns and far beyond the abilities of shore-based aircraft, especially in the fast-moving warfare of the Battle of the Pacific. It is interesting to note, however, that although naval aircraft development had reached a par and perhaps exceeded the abilities of certain classes of shore-based aircraft, the Royal Navy operated just one type from the first day of the Second World War until the last, the Fairey Swordfish bi-plane torpedo bomber.

However, developments on the hardware side of naval operations meant that the aircraft carrier did not have it all its own way in terms of technological advance. Radar had been a British development prior to the outbreak of war and by the later stages of the conflict almost every medium or large warship and some auxiliaries were equipped with radio ranging and direction which could be used for gunnery and air or search warning.

Below the water, asdic had been developed into active sonar, hull-mounted on escorts like the new breed of fast, well-equipped destroyers with new anti-submarine systems such as the forward-throwing hedgehog mortar. As always happens in naval or military development, one side of the 'battle' develops to keep pace with the other; thus, as destroyers and other anti-submarine weapons were developed, so the submarines themselves progressed.

Technology was introduced by the Germans which was a basic development of electronic warfare. When anti-submarine aircraft like RAF Coastal Command's Sunderlands or the carrier-launched Swordfish were fitted with anti-surface vessel radar, the submarines for which they were searching, usually at night, were equipped with a radar detector which allowed them either to prepare a hostile reception or to dive to safety before the attacker was in range with rockets or depth bombs.

Submarine development in the German Navy had been swift and almost deadly for the British because the sea life-line had almost been severed. But even in 1945, submarines still required to surface and re-charge their electric batteries, and then they became vulnerable to air and surface attack. The next development was the true submarine, which rarely needed to surface, and the Germans had begun work along those lines when the war ended. The victorious powers were also eager to obtain some of that technology for themselves, but not eager to share it. The Royal Navy was able to test, for some years, several German U-boat designs including the peroxide-drive *Meteor* before it became clear that the 'atomic' submarine was just around the corner.

**Above** *One of the central pillars of the Royal Navy's force structure is the nuclear-powered Fleet type submarine with the primary role of detecting and destroying enemy submarines. This is the returning* Conqueror *after the Falklands conflict (RN).*

**Below** Ark Royal, *the largest warship in the modern Royal Navy, seen with part of her air group ranged on deck. She has been built bearing in mind lessons learned in the early service life of her two sister ships (RN/Ark Royal).*

Atomic power for propulsion has given the submarine the ability to traverse great distances underwater with only the ability of the crew to keep functioning as a consideration for surfacing. By the late 1960s, especially with the development of submarine-launched ballistic missiles, the nuclear-armed submarine had begun to take the place of the aircraft carrier.

In the intervening 20 years, the aircraft carrier had nonetheless proved itself supremely capable of police actions and the landing of troops to project foreign policy decisions. The first action was Korea, where for more than three years the Royal Navy kept a fully functioning Light Fleet aircraft carrier on station some 12,000 miles from its home base. Later operations off Malaya and Borneo, Aden and East Africa were to show the ability of strike aircraft and troop-carrying helicopters to operate far from home. It was of course Suez which showed the ability of a naval force in the strike and landing roles; it was a good example of naval power even though it was not total victory because of political interference, good or bad.

Aircraft carriers needed protection, however, and by 1950 guided weapons were being rapidly developed to defend ships, especially the larger types against which the Japanese kamikazes had been so effective. The threat was now no longer from surface action but from air and submarine attack. Later, in the late 1970s, as missiles were developed to fly and home-in over the horizon, the surface threat reappeared, but the Royal Navy did not take the threat of sea-skimming missiles seriously until the sinking of *Sheffield* in the South Atlantic in 1982.

Today's warships are armed with a variety of guided weapons for anti-air defence against aircraft and missiles at long, medium and short ranges, irrespective of height. All warships, and perhaps soon the larger auxiliaries down to frigate size, are armed with Seacat, Sea Wolf or Sea Dart.

To counter surface targets, the Royal Navy purchased the French Exocet and more recently the American Harpoon (which is also used by submarines), but the automatic gun remains an important part of the integrated weapons systems aboard ship. Against the submarine, the mortar has given way to the stand-off Ikara torpedo-launcher, the ship-launched torpedo and the helicopter.

Rotary-winged aviation has revolutionized the Royal Navy, and helicopters have played a major role in all actions since Suez, where the first helicopter amphibious assault was carried out at Port Said. The helicopter has several roles today, including anti-submarine

warfare, anti-surface vessel warfare, commando assault and re-supply, search and rescue, and vertical replenishment; it has also taken over the airborne early warning radar role from the fixed-wing aircraft developed in the late 1940s. In the latter technology, the Royal Navy has again been a world leader.

In the late 1960s, the government of the day decided to bring the Royal Navy back from East of Suez and to concentrate its abilities on the Eastern Atlantic, Norwegian Sea and English Channel areas. This saw the demise of the fixed-wing aircraft carrier and the birth of the light aircraft carrier of the 'Invincible' Class, originally designed to take large numbers of medium-sized helicopters to sea and then given the Sea Harrier short take-off and vertical landing Fleet fighter. This aircraft, armed with the Sidewinder guided missile, was especially important in the Falklands campaign in 1982 and is subsequently being upgraded to meet the requirements of the 1990s, including the provision of the Sea Eagle anti-shipping missile.

**Above** *First of a new breed, the Sea King airborne early warning helicopter equipped with a powerful radar for detecting low-flying aircraft and missiles which threaten modern ships at sea (RN/Culdrose).*

**Right** *A workhorse of the modern Royal Navy, the Sea King HAS 5 (shown here lowering its Type 195M dipping sonar into the sea) is the main-stay of the airborne anti-submarine forces (RN/Gannet).*

**Left** *Sailors have always been the most important element of the Royal Navy and although high technology is now the watchword of the Service, tradition, such as 'colours', is still carefully preserved (RN/Drake).*

**Right** *Since 1945 there have been many changes to the Royal Dockyards, and by early 1987 there were only two remaining, both privatized, Plymouth Devonport and Rosyth, shown here during Navy Days (RN/FOSNI).*

Supporting the Royal Navy, the Royal Fleet Auxiliary Service has been developing in parallel with the warship and other weapons of the Fleet. The trend today is away from the single-role support ships — tankers, air stores, dry stores, etc — of the last 40 years and into the one-stop ship capable of providing everything needed for a warship to operate for three to five days. Every naval operation has been supported in one way or another by the RFA, none so much perhaps as the Falklands, but there are changes underway for the RFA as well, with the development of self-protection devices and other aids to survival in an increasingly hostile environment.

Perhaps the one thing which has not greatly changed in the Royal Navy is the sailor. Since the late 1950s, the Royal Navy, like the other British fighting services, has been all volunteer, and although at times it has been difficult to recruit and retain the qualified and skilled men needed in a modern warship, the standards have not been allowed to slip. The modern frigate and destroyer are fully automated wherever possible, requiring one-third of the men needed 30 years ago. Over the last few years, there has been an increase in the numbers of technical ratings, and new technical branches have been formed to cater for the weapons, sensors and other high-technology developments. One problem now, however, seems to be the longer time spent at sea — about 300 days a year — and the strain thus imposed on the married sailors and their officers.

The contraction of the Royal Navy since the 1950s has led to a decline in the number of Royal Dockyards, with the closure of Chatham and the downgrading of Portsmouth to the status of Fleet

Operating and Naval Base. Establishments have been rationalized over the last few years but the Falklands conflict ensured that not all the ill-conceived plans put forward in the 1981 Defence White Paper of the then Secretary of State for Defence, John Nott, have been carried out. There is continued concern within NATO, to which the United Kingdom makes the largest European naval contribution, about the number of anti-submarine warfare escorts and mines countermeasures vessels in the Royal Navy. In the past few years there has been commitment to 50 frigates and destroyers, but that figure is not guaranteed.

Amongst the Royal Navy's principal roles now is the protection and deployment of the United Kingdom's independent strategic deterrent by means of the nuclear-powered ballistic missile submarines carrying the Polaris system, which is scheduled to be replaced by Trident in the next decade. It is also charged with the defence of the United Kingdom and the protection of British interests worldwide as well as major maritime contributions to the Eastern Atlantic and English Channel sea areas, especially the anti-submarine protection of NATO striking forces and merchant shipping, and to world stability outside the NATO area.

Every year, the Royal Navy deploys ships to the Eastern Atlantic (including the Norwegian Sea), Northern Ireland waters, the North English Channel, Gibraltar, Hong Kong, the Gulf, the Falklands/South Atlantic, the West Indies and the Baltic Sea. Even so, the Royal Navy's 73,000 personnel (including the Royal Marines, Royal Fleet Auxiliary, Women's Royal Naval Service and Queen

Alexandra's Royal Naval Nursing Service) are third in the financial pecking order after the Royal Air Force and British Army, accounting for about £2,500 million annually as a combat force. Of this figure, nearly 50 per cent goes on equipment, 21 per cent on support services, 20 per cent on pay and pensions, 7 per cent on the Dockyards, privatized in April 1987, and 6 per cent on civilian pay outside the Dockyard organization.

In world terms, the Royal Navy is still the third most powerful (after the Soviet Union and the United States), but must be regarded as a top runner for professionalism and efficiency. When tested in the Falklands, some 8,000 miles from home, it certainly was not found lacking.

## LESSONS FROM THE FALKLANDS

Perhaps the most significant event in post-Second World War naval history was the Falklands conflict which took place in the South Atlantic between April and July 1982, following the invasion of the British colonies of South Georgia and the Falkland Islands by Argentine forces. Argentina had, and still has, a claim to sovereignty over these islands even though they are peopled by a predominantly farming population of British descent.

The day-by-day history of the Falklands conflict has been covered in detail by many authors, but the resultant changes to the Royal Navy are less well known and deserve some explanation.

**Below left** Hurworth, *one of four 'Hunt' Class MCMVs despatched to the Gulf in August 1987, receives one of two additional Oerlikon/BMARC 20mm KAA cannon for self-defence and mine destruction. Other equipment fitted included the Wallop Industries Barricade naval missile decoy system and MEL's Matilda electronic warfare equipment. Note the funnel badge of the 4th Mines Countermeasures Squadron – the Sooty Foot (RN/Danny du Feu).*

**Right** Hurworth *leads Bicester under the Forth Bridge into the North Sea for passage to Gibraltar and the Gulf (RN/Danny du Feu).*

Above all, the Falklands' liberation — Operation Corporate — was a significant and successful action 'Out of Area' and should not be taken as directly comparable with all the Royal Navy's daily tasks as part of the NATO Alliance, patrolling the North Atlantic, English Channel, North and Norwegian Seas. In the official British Government White Paper it has been described as 'unique' and the authors insist that caution be used when deciding what lessons were learned for future naval operations, warship design and training. However, there are lessons and developments which have come from the conflict which have affected the everyday life of naval personnel and will continue to influence future naval design. Some lessons related to the Royal Navy's continued ability to operate anywhere in the world, and had equal application to the everyday role of the modern Royal Navy as part of the NATO Alliance, where the primary role is the protection of shipping and conventional deterrence in the Eastern Atlantic.

In addition, immediately prior to Operation Corporate, the Royal Navy had been stung by the potential harsh cuts in its operational capability, including the scrapping of *Endurance* (which regularly visits the Falklands) and the amphibious assault ships *Fearless* and *Intrepid*, as proposed by the then Secretary of State for Defence, (Sir) John Nott in the 1981 Defence White Paper. In some ways, the South Atlantic conflict came as a godsend to overturn some of the more ill-conceived proposals, although as the success of Corporate recedes into history, and bearing in mind that politicians have very short memories when it suits them, the Royal Navy may again be facing severe cuts in its portion of the Defence vote.

Operation Corporate's overall command and control rested with the so-called War Cabinet, chaired by the Prime Minister and composed of several senior ministers, advised by the Chief of the Defence Staff, Admiral of the Fleet Lord Lewin, and other specialists. At sea, some 8,000 miles from the operational control centre at the Commander-in-Chief Fleet's headquarters at Northwood, through which the War Cabinet's orders were filtered, Flag Officer First Flotilla, Rear Admiral (now Admiral Sir Sandy) Woodward, commanded the carrier battle group and the

*Shipping in Falkland Sound during May 1982 immediately after the landings to liberate the Falkland Islands. This view, taken from* Yarmouth's *flight deck, includes* Intrepid *and the merchant ship* Norland.

amphibious task group which would recover the Falklands from the Argentine military government. His tasks included the need to combat the enemy, support operations from a sea base against that enemy dug in on the Falklands (including South Georgia) and prepare to operate aircraft and warships from the airfields and harbours of the captured British colony.

History has shown that Admiral Woodward was successful, but as a result of the considerable interest in the campaign, including some severe criticism of various facets of British naval policy, the British Government introduced some independent assessments of the performance of British equipment and personnel during the Operation. Amongst the most serious criticisms launched against the Royal Navy was the overall warship design process and the use of various materials in the construction of modern surface combat ships.

There has been considerable ill-informed discussion about the use of aluminium in the building of the Type 21 frigate, two of which, *Antelope* and *Ardent*, were lost to enemy air action at San Carlos. The two Type 42 destroyers lost, *Sheffield* and *Coventry*, had little of that metal in their superstructure but the former burned for several days after the fateful Exocet attack despite the fact that the critics of aluminium claimed that steel ships don't burn. Naval design has to contend with the problem of top-weight as modern electronic sensors require to be placed as high as possible on a ship, and the lighter the metal used the better. An independent review found that the use of aluminium was not a major contributory factor to the eventual fate of the Type 21s, although its use in companion ladders, hatches, etc was reviewed, to be directed against in future.

It is the use of other flammable or dangerous materials between decks which has been given the most attention, which is very right and proper because a remedy was easily prepared and could have the greatest effect in the shortest time.

Attention has also been given to the self-rescue devices in the companion-ways and compartments below deck, to the materials used in bunk-bed mattresses (only mines countermeasures vessels now have foam), and to the bulkhead and deckhead materials, where Formica-like substances were found to shatter easily if an explosion occurred, spreading needle-sharp fragments across a wide area causing death and maiming. The use of rubber-coated cables which give off toxic fumes has been stopped and most have been replaced. Any visitor to a post-Falklands warship cannot help but be impressed by the safety measures now taken, especially the Elsa breathing equipment at every corner.

Damage control proved a key to the successful efforts to save frigates hit by Argentine bombs. This has always been a key doctrine in the Royal Navy, and in 1987 a new trainer was opened at *Raleigh*, the naval training school, with plans to open others at Portsmouth and Rosyth. It will train about 6,000 men annually in all the arts and sciences of saving a damaged ship.

On the equipment side, weapons and sensors were found to be lacking. Too few ships were equipped with adequate self-defence weapons for sea-skimming missile protection, as shown by the sinking of *Sheffield* and *Atlantic Conveyor* to Exocet, and against low-flying aircraft using the cover of coastal hills, as in the case of *Coventry*, *Ardent*, *Antelope* and the five other warships damaged during air attacks.

Moving target indication for air warning radar has been improved and new designs have better close-in protection. In fact, within weeks of the beginning of the conflict, *Illustrious*, the second of the new class of light aircraft carriers, had been fitted with the American-designed Phalanx rotary cannon, and since then *Invincible* has also been fitted with additional 20 mm Oerlikon guns and special launchers for flare, chaff and other decoys against aircraft and missile threats.

British warships of the last two to three decades were not designed to operate in confined waters such as those found in the San Carlos area, where they were almost sitting ducks against the determined air attacks from the Argentine naval air arm and air force. With such difficult operational conditions, especially for combat air patrols, it was a major disadvantage not to have airborne early warning assistance from an organic source — one embarked aboard ships in the Task Force. The Royal Navy had been without airborne early warning since the demise of the Gannet in 1978, and this lack was certainly a major cause in the sinking of *Sheffield* (on picket duty) and may have contributed to the sinking of *Sir Galahad* at Bluff Coves. The lack of battlefield support helicopters (several sank in *Atlantic Conveyor*) was also a contributory factor in the latter loss. Within weeks of the conflict ending, the first Sea King airborne early warning helicopters were being tested in the South Atlantic, proof of the amazing speed with which British military, civil service and industrial concerns can operate in an emergency — another lesson re-learned in the Falklands.

British shipbuilders were also able to complete the light aircraft carrier *Illustrious* ahead of schedule and she was being made ready to go south and relieve *Invincible* when hostilities ceased; she was deployed in September 1982, the first British warship for many years to go to war without a formal commissioning ceremony.

Since the late 1970s and the advent of the anti-shipping missile, the naval gun had fallen into the category of welcome but not necessary. The Falklands proved that was wrong. Naval gunfire support is a useful addition to aerial attack and the ability of warships to pass close inshore during the hours of darkness and continue to bombard enemy troop positions has a definite effect on morale. Yet, the latest and best defensively equipped warships in the South Atlantic in 1982, the Type 22 frigates armed with Sea Wolf, were not able to take part because their only guns were the close-in 40 mm Bofors. By the time that the next Defence White Paper had been presented to the British Parliament, the new generation of Batch 3 Type 22 and Type 23 frigates had been re-designed to incorporate the Vickers 4.5 in (114 mm) gun which had proved so useful in South Georgia, the Falkland Islands and Southern Thule.

Considerable acclaim was won by the Fleet Air Arm during the conflict, especially by the Sea Harrier fighters which managed to maintain a presence, although not complete air superiority, during most of the campaign. These aircraft operated mainly from the aircraft carriers which had to be kept offshore, away from Falklands or mainland-based enemy strike aircraft which, had they sunk an aircraft carrier, would have scored a considerable blow against British morale; also because of the importance of such a ship, such a loss would undoubtedly have won the conflict for Argentina.

As a result of the conflict, the squadron allocation of Sea Harriers has risen to eight (rather than five) and three Sea King AEW 2s are carried in addition to the anti-submarine warfare models of this helicopter. *Ark Royal* was completed with Falklands lessons for below-deck storage and workshop areas taken into consideration, and the other two 'Invincible' Class CVSs will be refitted in due course.

The Sea Kings in fact bore the brunt of the ASW effort, and although neither of their parent aircraft carriers, *Hermes* and *Invincible*, were successfully engaged by Argentine submarines, it is obvious that even the world's best medium ASW helicopter with the best-trained crews found tracking the ultra-quiet conventional submarines a major problem. Since then, all Royal Navy ASW helicopter squadrons have been equipped with the Mk 5 version, but the difficulty in tracking these submarines is a continual problem for the Fleet Air Arm in the Eastern Atlantic, especially as the Soviets' latest nuclear-powered vessels are regarded as ultra-quiet as well.

The supporting Royal Fleet Auxiliaries proved that they could keep the Fleet supplied over a protracted time and distance from the home base, although many are now sprouting defensive weapons and active countermeasure systems. The time remaining for the RFA to remain a merchant service must now be limited; like the surface combat ships, RFAs find the small-calibre weapon has its attractions for close-in defence.

Although many of the more important lessons have been implemented and many of the 1981 White Paper findings overturned, the Royal Navy is again finding its budget cut despite an increasingly important role in the defence of Western Europe with anti-submarine operations in the Eastern Atlantic and the support of the Northern Flank. The Trident programme, which is designed to replace Polaris, the nuclear strategic and independent deterrent, and the safeguarding of which is a key RN role, must be playing its

Yarmouth *returns from the South Atlantic to Rosyth, her base port, to the waiting cheers of relatives and friends* (RN/FOSNI).

part in the paring down of naval spending. Ships are spending longer at sea and this is causing retention problems in certain skill categories and ever increasing costs; especially in keeping pace with sensor and weapon technology, and these will take their toll on the desperate need to replace the older frigates.

If the Falklands conflict proved anything, it was that the Royal Navy is a highly trained, professional force with a flexible command and control structure second to none in the world. Despite defence cuts and relatively little active service, the Royal Navy has the capability of deployment almost anywhere to support any military or foreign policy task. Such a role is valuable in the pursuit of world peace.

## ARMILLA PATROL

As a result of increased tension in the Arabian Gulf, the British Government despatched four 'Hunt' Class MCMVs — *Brecon* and *Brocklesby* (1st Mines Countermeasures Squadron) with *Bicester* and *Hurworth* (MCM 4) — and the support ship *Abdiel* to the Gulf in August 1987. The presence of mines of various types prompted this move to protect both British warships and merchantmen in international waters. RFA *Diligence*, from the Falklands, was also deployed, together with RFA *Regent* (complete with Wessex helicopter) to join the Armilla Patrol.

These craft joined the existing warships, usually a frigate and a guided missile destroyer, which have been stationed around the Straits of Hormuz since just after the commencement of hostilities between Iran and Iraq. The warships, together with a Royal Fleet Auxiliary tanker, have been stationed there to accompany British and Commonwealth merchant ships through the difficult passage to Kuwait and the United Arab Emirates.

# COMMAND, CONTROL and ORGANIZATION

## SENIOR COMMAND

The Royal Navy is Britain's senior service, but is fully integrated into the tri-service defence structure. The Queen is the titular head of the service as Lord High Admiral, but operational command rests in the hands of the Chief of the Defence Staff and Defence Council. The Council, as adviser to the Prime Minister, is chaired by the UK's Secretary of State for Defence, and the chief of the Naval Staff is one of its primary advisers.

Next in the reporting order is the Admiralty Board, the policy-making body of the Royal Navy, at the head of which sits the Secretary of State for Defence, again acting as chairman. Its role is to advise the Government of the day, through the Defence Council, on maritime affairs and policy, using the accumulated expertise of the First Sea Lord (Chief of the Naval Staff), the Second Sea Lord (who is also Chief of Naval Personnel), the Controller of the Navy and the Chief of Fleet Support. In addition to these uniformed members who sit on the Board are two civil servants, the Second Permanent Under Secretary of State and the Controller of Research and Development Establishments.

The Chief of the Naval Staff, who has direct access to the Prime Minister if needs be, chairs the Executive Committee of the Admiralty Board, which effectively runs the everyday affairs of the Royal Navy.

Warships and similar assets come under the everyday control of Commander-in-Chief Fleet (CINCFLEET) at his headquarters at Northwood, Middlesex, just to the north-west of London. All operational warships and the Polaris submarines come under his control, the latter directly without any subordinate commanders. He is one of the three senior NATO commanders, wearing the NATO 'hat' of Allied Commander-in-Chief Channel and Commander-in-Chief Eastern Atlantic. However, he is not alone in his national and Alliance responsibilities as many Flag Officers (so-called because when they are resident at sea or ashore their flag is worn by the ship or establishment) have dual roles.

Based at Portsmouth, the other British national Commander-in-Chief is the Admiral responsible for Naval Home Command

The First Sea Lord Britain's senior sailor and, by selection, Chief of the Defence Staff. The First Sea Lord (known as 1SL in the service) also carries the titles of Chief of the Naval Staff and First & Principal Naval Aide-de-Camp to the Queen. Since August 1985, the post has been held by Admiral Sir William Staveley GCB ADC who joined the Royal Navy as a cadet in 1942. His senior appointments include command of the 6th Minesweeper squadron, the frigate Zulu, the assault ship Intrepid, the Commando carrier Albion and Flag Officer Second Flotilla. In 1980, on promotion to Vice Admiral, he was appointed Vice Chief of the Naval Staff and later Commander-in-Chief Fleet.

Commander-in-Chief *The senior operational command post in the Royal Navy, the role of CINCFLEET carries with it the NATO commands of Allied Commander-in-Chief Channel and Eastern Atlantic Area. The post has been held since May 1987 by Admiral Sir Julian Oswald KCB , who trained as a gunnery officer including service in the Royal Navy's last battleship, Vanguard. His seagoing commands have included the minesweeper Yarnton, the frigate Bacchante and the destroyer Newcastle. His staff jobs have included Assistant Chief of the Defence Staff (Programmes), Captain of the Britannia Royal Naval College, Dartmouth, and recently Flag Officer Third Flotilla. CINCFLEET is an important senior command in the British armed forces and any officer aspiring to the job must show an extraordinary ability in the various command and staff appointments during his career. As with all senior posts, a certain amount of flair is needed making it impossible to set any pattern for a career path to the top; it is individual ability which counts in command jobs in the RN (RN).*

(CINCNAVHOME) who commands the various training and depot establishments around the United Kingdom, as well as the Royal Naval Reserve. It is his role to provide the trained manpower for CINCFLEET to use operationally, and he is also responsible for the naval participation in the defence of the United Kingdom.

Afloat there are three Flag Officers for the operational warships:

**Above** CINCFLEET's command centre control room at Northwood, which is also the headquarters of Channel and Eastern Atlantic NATO commands. Officers and other ranks present are looking at a large display with the position of warships and other assets of friendly and not so friendly nations (RN).

Admiral Sir John Woodward KCB Vice Admiral Sandy Woodward commanded the Task Force sent to the South Atlantic in 1982 as Flag Officer First Flotilla, with the rank of Rear Admiral. A submariner by specialization, Admiral Woodward was appointed Flag Officer Submarines in May 1983, promoted Vice Admiral in September 1984 (as in this picture) and Admiral in July 1987, becoming Commander-in-Chief Naval Home Command (RN).

Flag Officer First Flotilla *Responsible for the type command destroyer and frigate force of the Royal Navy and acting as deputy to CINCFLEET, he is known by the abbreviation FOF1. Vice Admiral John Kerr trained as a navigation specialist and was commanding officer of the aircraft carrier* Illustrious, *the frigate* Achilles *and the destroyer* Birmingham. *Under the new command structure for flotilla flag officers, the training carried out at Portland by Flag Officer Sea Training (see page 31) is on his behalf and FOST reports to FOF1 rather than CINCFLEET in this respect (RN).*

Flag Officer Naval Air Command *Responsible for providing serviceable aircraft and trained personnel in war and peace, FONAC has his headquarters at Yeovilton. Rear Admiral Roger Dimmock, a pilot by training, assumed the post in 1987 after many years in the Fleet Air Arm, which included flying Scimitars and Buccaneers, before commanding the frigate* Naiad, *RNAS Culdrose and the aircraft carrier* Hermes.

Flag Officer First Flotilla (FOF1) has type command of all destroyers and frigates, and Flag Officer Second Flotilla (FOF2) has Out of Area command for the Gulf, Caribbean and South Atlantic, as well as exercises and deployments. The ships are divided into frigate and destroyer squadrons for the implementation of national and NATO maritime policy. Flag Officer Third Flotilla (FOF 3) is the large ship, amphibious task group and naval aviation afloat commander to whom Flag Officer Naval Air Command (FONAC) supplies aircraft and their crews. Flag Officer Royal Yachts is the only Admiral in direct command of a warship, and operates from afloat in HMY *Britannia*.

Two of the three area flag officers have NATO sea areas under their responsibility in addition to their role of administering shore establishments on behalf of CINCNAVHOME. Flag Officer Plymouth is responsible for the ships in the Plymouth Sea Area, running from the southern North Sea, through the English Channel to the Eastern Atlantic as far as the coast of Mauritania and including the southern Irish Sea and the South-West Approaches. Further north, and with control of naval shipping to Greenland and the Norwegian Coast, Flag Officer Scotland and Northern Ireland

*Flag Officer Scotland & Northern Ireland From 1985 to 1987, the appointment of FOSNI was held by Vice Admiral Sir George Vallings KCB, a former Commodore Clyde and Flag Officer Gibraltar. Admiral Vallings served in the aircraft carrier Theseus during the Korean war, commanded the 'Daring' Class fleet escort Defender, the Second Frigate Squadron and the frigate Apollo. As FOSNI he is one of two senior sea area commanders with NATO roles as well as national interests to safeguard.*

(FOSNI), based near Rosyth naval base, is also a land area commander. Apart from direct war roles, FOSNI is responsible for the protection of British offshore interests in the North Sea, Irish Sea and North Atlantic, including Fishery Protection and offshore hydrocarbons.

Flag Officer Plymouth has the NATO roles of Commander Central Sub-Area Eastern Atlantic and Plymouth Sub-Area Channel, whilst FOSNI wears the NATO 'hats' of Commander Northern Sub-Area Eastern Atlantic and Sub-Area Channel. Flag Officer Submarines, who controls the British conventional and nuclear-powered Fleet type submarines, also undertakes the duties of the NATO Commander Submarines Eastern Atlantic.

Surprisingly, Flag Officer Portsmouth has a subordinate sea area commander role to Plymouth Command, and no NATO role. His land area command is, however, large with a number of important establishments in the Portsmouth area and the important Fleet operating facilities in the old Dockyard, which are under the control of the Chief of Fleet Support.

Other important national commanders include the Flag Officers Gibraltar (with a NATO role in protecting the Straits of Gibraltar),

Flag Officer Submarines *Not only does the Flag Officer Submarines (FOSM) have control of all the non-strategic submarines in the Royal Navy, but he is also Allied Commander Submarines Eastern Atlantic for NATO. Rear Admiral Frank Grenier joined the Royal Navy from school, commanding the submarine* Ambush *in 1965. Late he was appointed executive officer of* Resolution, *the first Polaris submarine, during her first commission and later ran the 'Perishers' course at Faslane for future submarine COs. He commanded the guided missile destroyer* Liverpool, *and worked on the Trident programme before moving to Portsmouth as Chief of Staff to CINCNAVHOME. He was appointed FOSM in May 1987.*

Flag Officer Sea Training *This is one of the most important appointments in NATO and provides the Royal Navy and many European navies with the ability to fulfil the capabilities of their warships and ships' companies. Rear Admiral Barry Wilson was the Flag Officer in charge of sea training facility at Portland from 1985 to 1987. Before taking up his appointment he was Navigating Officer of Eagle and Commanding Officer of both Mohawk and Cardiff (RN/Osprey).*

Commodore Minor War Vessels & Fisheries Protection *This relatively new post combines the needs of the Fishery Protection squadron and the various offshore patrol vessels around the British coast. The first officer in the post is Commodore Barry Clarke, a navigation specialist and former commanding officer of the frigates Malcolm and Ariadne. Other appointments include Chief Staff Officer to the Commander Standing Naval Force Atlantic, Defence & Naval Attache to the Netherlands and the last Captain Fishery Protection (RN/FOSNI).*

Sea Training and the Hydrographer to the Navy. Below the ranks of Admiral, Vice Admiral and Rear Admiral are the posts to which senior Captains are appointed as Commodores (one thick gold ring is the mark of this appointment), including Minor War Vessels, Amphibious Warfare and Clyde.

# WARSHIP SQUADRONS

For many years, the Royal Navy has used the flotilla and squadron system to provide the subordinate structure of the command and organizational functions of warships at sea. In February 1988, the command structure changed to bring all nine destroyer and frigate squadrons under the type command of Flag Officer First Flotilla and the operational and tactical command under Flag Officer Second Flotilla. In addition, there are five squadrons of mines counter-measures vessels, four of patrol vessels (for the Falklands, Hong Kong, Northern Ireland, Fishery Protection and surveying) and four of submarines, including the Polaris boats.

## FIRST FLOTILLA

| | |
|---|---|
| First Frigate Squadron (F1) | 'Leander' Class Batch 1 (Ikara) |
| Second Frigate Squadron (F2) | Type 22 Batch 1 |
| Third Destroyer Squadron (D3) | Type 42 Batch 1 |
| Fourth Frigate Squadron (F4) | Type 21 |
| Fifth Destroyer Squadron (D5) | Type 42 Batch 2 |
| Sixth Frigate Squadron (F6) | Type 12 Mod & 'Leander' Class Batch 3 |
| Seventh Frigate Squadron (F7) | 'Leander' Class Batch 2 (Exocet) |
| Eighth Frigate Squadron (F8) | 'Leander' Class Batch 3 (Seawolf) |
| Ninth Frigate Squadron (F9) | Type 22 Batch 2/3 |

## THIRD FLOTILLA

| | |
|---|---|
| Invincible | Fearless |
| Illustrious | Intrepid |
| Ark Royal | Bristol |

## SUBMARINE COMMAND

First Submarine Squadron
Second Submarine Squadron
Third Submarine Squadron
Tenth Submarine Squadron

## MINOR WAR VESSELS AND FISHERY PROTECTION

| | |
|---|---|
| Mines counter-measures | Minor war vessels |
| First MCM Squadron | Fishery Protection Squadron |
| Second MCM Squadron | |
| Third MCM Squadron | Hong Kong Patrol Squadron |
| Fourth MCM Squadron | Falkland Islands Patrol Squadron |
| Tenth MCM Squadron | Northern Ireland Squadron |

## SURVEY FLOTILLA

All Survey vessels

**Above** HMS Exeter, the first Type 42 guided missile destroyer to be armed with the American 20 mm Vulcan Phalanx close-in weapon system. This system, already fitted to the 'Invincible' Class aircraft carriers, is said to be capable of destroying sea-skimming missiles (Rolls-Royce).

**Below** Off to the Gulf. Two of the four British mine warfare vessels leave Rosyth for minehunting operations in the Arabian Sea and Persian Gulf. Leading is HMS Bicester (RN/PO Phot Danny du Feu).

**Above** *For many young would-be technicians, naval life begins the hard way with an assault course at HMS Collingwood, one of the several shore training establishments near Portsmouth (RN).*

**Above right** *Providing valuable sea time for the Royal Naval Reserve is a 'River' Class minesweeper; this is HMS Waveney in a moderate sea. The 'Rivers' use sweep or influence mine-clearing equipment (COI).*

**Right** *Snooping on the NATO warships during Exercise 'Ocean Safari 87', this Soviet naval aviation Cub electronic intelligence aircraft was intercepted, identified and shadowed by two Sea Harrier FRS 1s of 800 Naval Air Squadron, one of which took this picture.*

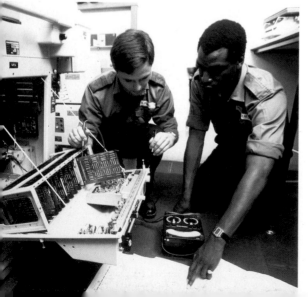

**Left** *Engineering Technicians (known to the Royal Navy as Artificers) working together to repair a piece of naval equipment. The high technology of the modern Royal Navy calls for very high calibre personnel at all levels (COI).*

**Right** One of the older nuclear-powered Fleet submarines (SSNs) is HMS Valiant. She is rarely found on the surface and spends most of her life patrolling in Atlantic and Norwegian waters, although British SSNs travel far afield, including a regular patrol to the South Atlantic (COI).

**Above** The Royal Marines Band Service provides the music and pageantry for the modern Royal Navy, but in wartime these smartly dressed men will become the medical orderlies of the Royal Marines — as they did during the Falklands conflict (COI).

**Below** Example and Explorer of the Royal Naval Auxiliary Service working together off the south coast of England. The RNAS provides a vital back-up service for the Royal Navy in time of war, having some responsibilities for ports and harbours with the Naval Ports Organization (COI).

Squadron Commanding Officer A rather unusual command appointment is that of the independent airborne early warning flights of 849 Squadron which currently operate Sea King AEW 2 helicopters from the 'Invincible' Class aircraft carriers. From 1985 to 1987, Lieutenant Commander Phil Howarth held the appointment of Commanding Officer 849A Flight. Commander Howarth is an observer by training, having been an AEW specialist from fixed-wing carriers in Gannet aircraft before a series of exchange staff appointments. He took command of 849A Flt when it worked up prior to embarking in Illustrious for the first operational testing of the concept (RN/Culdrose).

A frigate or destroyer squadron is commanded by a senior Captain Royal Navy — Captain F or Captain D depending on type of warship — with a small staff to administer the other ships, a job which is now particularly time consuming because they rarely operate together. It does, however, allow ships of the same class to be administered and experience has shown that improvements to design and operations result in this way.

Staff are appointed to a squadron for specific duties, like the Squadron Medical Officer, whilst others have a squadron appointment in addition to a position on the 'leader', such as Squadron Aviation Officer, who is usually the senior Flight Commander in the squadron embarked in the 'leader'. Until the Falklands conflict, a 'leader' was identified by a broad funnel top band and the 'half-leader' by a narrow band. Often the squadron number is worn on the side of the funnel or in some other conspicuous position.

Smaller ship squadrons, the so-called Minor War Vessels, have senior Lieutenant Commanders as commanders of such units. The Tenth Mines Countermeasures Squadron is made up of Royal Naval Reserve-manned ships with an integrated war role with the rest of the Royal Navy.

# INDIVIDUAL WARSHIPS

Aboard ship, the command structure has altered little in the last 100 years. The commanding officer — always called the captain irrespective of his rank — can either be a Lieutenant Royal Navy (on some mines countermeasures vessels and conventional submarines), a Lieutenant Commander (larger minor war vessels), a Commander (most frigates and destroyers) or a 'four-ringed' Captain Royal Navy (usually for a squadron appointment or a large warship).

Everyday running of the ship is in the hands of the First Lieutenant or the Executive Officer, which for a larger ship is a Commander but which in smaller ships is frequently the First Lieutenant himself, or 'Jimmy'. Each warship is divided into departments — weapons engineering, aviation, supply and secretarial, etc.

On an aircraft carrier, the heads of department are Commanders with a number of other officers below them in a chain of command which ensures the smooth functioning of all onboard ship routines, including emergency actions. Each department has a number of divisions for the ratings, with an officer as the division officer who is responsible for the general welfare and discipline of his men. Larger ships also have full-time 'police', the ship's regulators, who prevent or investigate crime, but punishment is meted out by the commanding officer.

Like all professional services, the Royal Navy has its rank structure of officer, non-commissioned officer and rating. Each class of sailor is generally segregated from the other by centuries of ritual authority precedent. It is possible, however, to pass up through the ranks to become an officer, and today as many as 40 per cent of any ship's officers have been lower deck men selected for special duties or specially-trained 'upper yardmen' who go on to have full naval careers as officers. The rank structure ensures that in any given situation, each man will know how to behave and how to react, particularly important in action.

# SPECIALIST BRANCHES

The modern Royal Navy is divided into five specialist branches to service all the needs of a professional and high-technology naval force, and in which ratings from Junior Rating to Warrant Officer serve:

Operations Branch — divided into Seaman and Communications
 Groups
Engineering Branch — marine, weapon or air
Supply & Secretariat Branch
Medical Branch
Air Branch — the Fleet Air Arm

In addition, there are several branches which recruit from within the
five main branches as it is not possible for ratings, for example, to
join as submariners although ratings in several categories can
volunteer for selection; likewise divers, who are selected from the
Operations Branch. Both the Regulating Branch, responsible for a
wide range of disciplinary and administrative duties, and the
Physical Training Branch, take recruits from within the Royal Navy.

## OPERATIONS BRANCH
### Seaman Group
These ratings carry out the fighting and working of a warship at sea
and are given specialist training in a range of sub-specializations
including Electronic Warfare, Radar, Missile, Sonar (surface ships),

*Amongst the specialist tasks undertaken by the Operations Branch is diving and here
members of Drake's Clearance Diving Team carry out training drills in the
establishment's swimming pool (RN/Drake).*

Sonar (submarines), Diver, Mine Warfare, Survey Recorder and Tactical Systems (submarines). These are a ship's Operations Room workers, feeding data to and carrying out orders from the Command Team, headed by the Captain and his Principal Warfare Officer(s).

## Communications Group

A warship's communications suite is constantly at work and requires operators to send messages via Morse key, voice, flashing light and radio/satellite teletype. It is a constantly changing world. Sub-specialities are Radio Operator (tactical), Radio Operator (submarines) and Radio Operator (general).

## ENGINEERING BRANCH

There are three primary sub-specializations in this Branch and all are technology based. They are Marine Engineering (to provide power to move and arm a warship and for everyday running), Weapon Engineering (for the 'eyes', 'ears' and 'teeth' of the warship, divided into ordnance and radio) and Air Engineering (for fixed-wing and helicopter aviation support).

The Royal Navy's most highly-skilled ratings are the Artificers who are qualified to work on all the high-technology systems in a warship or shore establishment. As well as being first class

technicians, Artificers are men and systems managers. Ratings can be selected for Artificer training or join directly after an appropriate engineering apprenticeship in a civilian job.

## SUPPLY & SECRETARIAT BRANCH
The five sub-specializations in this Branch are all directly connected with maintaining the warship's administration and smooth running. The skills are Cook, Steward, Catering Accountant, Stores Accountant and Writer.

## MEDICAL BRANCH
Medical Assistants and Medical Technicians are the sub-specializations in this Branch, the former assisting with the fitness of naval personnel and the latter with specialist skills such as physiotherapy, radiography, dispensing, health inspection and laboratory work.

## AIR BRANCH
Ratings can join the Fleet Air Arm as naval airmen to work on the flight decks of modern warships and ashore at the naval air stations to control, direct and position aircraft. Professional progress includes training for aircraft handling, driving, survival equipment and

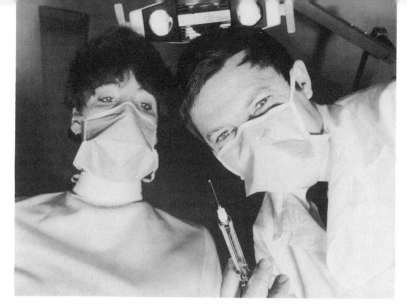

**Above** *The modern Royal Navy boasts a professional medical service with medical and dental officers and rating assistants. Drake's dentist with his Wren dental assistant prepare a patient for treatment (RN/Drake).*

**Below** *Ratings at Collingwood, one of several training establishments in the United Kingdom. This is the traditional procedure of 'off caps', tutored by a Petty Officer (RN).*

meteorology. The majority of the naval photographers are from this Branch.

In 1985, published figures showed that new recruits could expect to go to sea an average of six months after enlistment, having passed through satisfactory initial training at *Raleigh* in South Devon.

| Sub-specialization | Training establishment | First time at sea |
|---|---|---|
| Electronic Warfare | *Dryad* | 7 months |
| Radar | *Dryad* | 7 months |
| Missile | *Cambridge* | 6 months |
| Sonar | *Dryad* or *Dolphin* | 7 months |
| Diver | Vernon/Portsmouth | 8 months |
| Mine Warfare | Vernon/*Dryad* | 6 months |
| Survey Recorder | Hydrographic School | 4 months |
| Tactical Systems | *Dolphin* | 6 months |
| Radio Operator | *Mercury* | 9 months |
| Radio Operator (sub) | *Mercury* | 12 months |
| Engineering Mechanic | *Sultan* | 5 months |
| Weapon Mechanic | *Collingwood* | 8 months |
| Air Mechanic | *Daedalus* | 24 months |
| Cook | Aldershot | 10 months |
| Steward | *Raleigh* | 6 months |
| Catering Accountant | *Raleigh* | 15 months |
| Stores Accountant | *Raleigh* | 14 months |
| Writer | *Raleigh* | 30 months |
| Medical Assistant | *Haslar* | 36 months |
| Medical Technician | *Haslar* | no figures |
| Naval Airman | *Seahawk/Daedalus* | 12 months |

# PROMOTION FOR RATINGS

**Junior Rate** Enters the Royal Navy at 16 and after successful training will advance at 17½ years to Ordinary Rate.

**Able Rate** According to category and subject to passing tests, the Ordinary Rate will advance to this rate after 9 to 12 months.

**Leading Rate** Advancement to this rate is at 22 to 23 years.

**Petty Officer** The first non-commissioned rate is by advancement in trade or skill at about 26 to 28 years old.

**Chief Petty Officer** Promotion to Chief Petty Officer is by seniority, recommendation and selection in the early to mid 30s.

**Warrant Officer** Formerly called Fleet Chief Petty Officer, this rate, which is that of the Queen's warrant, is by selection on the basis of qualifications and service record. Warrant Officers serve until at least 45 years and naturally are the most respected members of the Lower Deck.

Chief Petty Officer *The senior non-commissioned officer rank in the Royal Navy. CPOs are long-servicing and experienced ratings, such as CPO Gunnery Instructor Mackenzie BEM, one of the training team at the Naval Gunnery School at* Cambridge, *near Plymouth (RN).*

## OFFICER SELECTION

**Direct Entry** This is based on educational qualifications and the ability to complete the Admiralty Interview Board at *Sultan*; for the Fleet Air Arm, there is an additional test for aptitude at RAF Biggin Hill. Initial training is performed at the Britannia Royal Naval College, Dartmouth.

**Upper Yardman** Ratings are selected with 5 or more O levels for Full or Short Service commissions, with eventual promotion to at least Lieutenant Commander and some to Commander and higher. At least one rating in post-war RN history has become a full Admiral.

**Special Duties** This career path allows longer service as a rating, taking account of experience and knowledge, with selection to Petty Officer at between 25 and 34, before commissioning to Sub-Lieutenant and a further career in a specialist role.

Officer ranks are: Admiral of the Fleet; Admiral; Vice Admiral;

*Splice the main brace: Warrant Officers and Chief Petty Officers 'up spirits' on a special occasion. WO Coxswain R.R. Commoes is acting Rum Bosun in traditional 19th century dress. Despite some old traditions proudly carried on, today's Royal Navy is a modern, forward looking service (7N/Illustrious).*

Rear Admiral; Commodore; Captain; Commander; Lieutenant Commander; Lieutenant; Sub-Lieutenant; Midshipman.

## OFFICER SPECIALIZATION

Although Royal Naval officers are trained as professionals, they are also trained as specialists as part of the network of independent branches to which the ratings belong. All make a vital contribution to the whole and the Royal Navy could not function as the world's most professional naval service without these specializations.

**Seaman Officer** The fundamental officer responsible for the working and fighting of a ship, leading to Command. Generally a Full Career specialization but also with a fair proportion of Short Service officers, who can sub-specialize in Aircraft Control, Aviation (pilot or observer), Mine Warfare & Clearance Diving, Submarines and Hydrographic Surveying. Only Seaman Officers have command of ships, squadrons and flotillas.

**Engineer Officer** A diverse area with five sub-specializations of a highly technical background: Weapons Engineer (surface ships), Weapons Engineer (submarines), Marine Engineer (surface ships), Marine Engineer (submarines) and Air Engineer (Mechanical & Electrical).

**Supply & Secretariat Officer** A large and varied branch which deals with pay, stores, catering and the direct support of Command in a secretarial role handling official correspondence and administration, including classified documents.

**Instructor Officer** A specialist teacher and man manager who ensures that naval personnel are abreast of the current and future trends in technology, as well as ensuring the continued advancement of all ranks. 'Schoolies', as they are known, also provide provide Meteorological and Oceanographical Officers to the Royal Navy. Other specialist areas include nuclear propulsion, training technology and automatic data processing.

## CAREER STEPS

Joining as a Midshipman at between 17 and 26 or as a Sub-Lieutenant between 19 and 26, the naval officer can expect to be a Lieutenant between 22 and 34, a Lieutenant Commander between 30 and 36, a Commander between 33 and 40, a Captain at about 45 (some have been as young as 37 in recent years) and a Rear Admiral at 50, rising to Admiral in the early to mid 50s. In some branches, promotion is limited to Rear Admiral or Vice Admiral by the smallness of the Branch. Promotion beyond Lieutenant Commander is by special selection, and competition beyond Captain is significant. The rank of Commodore is honorary for specific tasks, including Minor War Vessels, Amphibious Warfare and Clyde (for the submarine flotilla there).

# SEA POWER

Since the late 1960s, the submarine has replaced the aircraft carrier as the capital ship of the Royal Navy. This is mainly because of the emphasis given to the submarine building programme as Britain adopted nuclear-powered propulsion but also because it was perceived that the Royal Navy could no longer afford to keep pace with the developments in conventional fixed-wing naval aviation without jeopardizing the completely balanced nature of the Fleet.

## SUBMARINES

There are three types of submarine in service with the modern Royal Navy: nuclear-powered attack submarines; nuclear-powered ballistic missile carrying submarines; and diesel-electric attack submarines.

| Name | Pennant number | Flt Deck Code | Commissioned |
|------|------|------|------|
| **ATTACK SUBMARINES (SSN)** | | | |
| 'TRAFALGAR' CLASS' | | | |
| Trafalgar | S107 | | 27 May 1983 |
| Turbulent | S110 | | 28 April 1984 |
| Tireless | S117 | | 5 October 1985 |
| Torbay | S118 | | 7 February 1987 |
| Trenchant | S 91 | | 1988 |
| Talent | S 92 | | 1989 |
| Triumph | S 93 | | 1990 |
| 'SWIFTSURE' CLASS | | | |
| Swiftsure | S126 | | 17 April 1973 |
| Sovereign | S108 | | 11 July 1974 |
| Superb | S109 | | 13 November 1976 |
| Sceptre | S104 | | 14 February 1978 |
| Spartan | S105 | | 22 September 1979 |
| Splendid | S106 | | 21 March 1981 |
| 'CHURCHILL' CLASS | | | |
| Churchill | S 46 | | 15 July 1970 |
| Courageous | S 50 | | 16 October 1971 |
| Conqueror | S 48 | | 9 November 1971 |
| 'VALIANT' CLASS | | | |
| Valiant | S102 | | 18 July 1966 |
| Warspite | S103 | | 18 April 1967 |

**Above** Reckoned to be one of the quietest nuclear-propelled submarines in the world, Turbulent is the second of the 'Trafalgar' Class Fleet type submarines being built by Vickers at Barrow-in-Furness. This class is being equipped with the Marconi Spearfish torpedo and the Sub-Harpoon anti-shipping missile (RN/Gannet).

**Above right** In order to maintain the effectiveness of the older conventional submarines, the Royal Navy has installed a new bow-mounted sonar on some of the 'Oberon' Class boats which now form a separate class under the designation 'Opossum' Class after the first to be modified, seen here (Mike Lennon).

## PATROL SUBMARINES (SS/SSK)

### 'OBERON' CLASS

| | | |
|---|---|---|
| Odin | S10 | 3 May 1962 |
| Olympus | S12 | 7 July 1962 |
| Onslaught | S14 | 14 August 1962 |
| Oracle | S16 | 14 February 1963 |
| Otus | S18 | 5 October 1963 |
| Ocelot | S17 | 31 January 1964 |
| Opportune | S20 | 29 December 1964 |
| Onyx | S21 | 20 November 1967 |

### 'OPOSSUM' CLASS

| | | |
|---|---|---|
| Otter | S15 | 20 August 1962 |
| Osiris | S13 | 11 January 1964 |
| Opossum | S19 | 5 June 1964 |

### 'TYPE' 2400

| | | |
|---|---|---|
| Upholder | S40 | 1988 |
| Unseen | S41 | 1988 |
| Ursula | S42 | 1989 |
| Unicorn | S43 | 1989 |

## BALLISTIC MISSILE CARRYING SUBMARINE (SSBN)

'R' CLASS

| | | |
|---|---|---|
| Resolution | S22 | 2 October 1967 |
| Repulse | S23 | 28 September 1968 |
| Renown | S26 | 15 November 1968 |
| Revenge | S27 | 4 December 1969 |

'TRIDENT' CLASS

| | | |
|---|---|---|
| Vanguard | S? | 1990 |
| Vengeance | S? | |
| Victorious | S? | |
| Venerable | S? | |

Nuclear-powered attack submarines (SSNs) are used for a wartime role of seek and destroy, the target being enemy submarines (including ballistic missile and cruise missile carriers) and surface ships. They could also conceivably be used to protect friendly ballistic missile carrying submarines. In any naval task group, the nuclear-powered submarine, with its high endurance and submerged speed, is a useful asset to the group commander.

The modern Royal Navy operates four classes from the latest 'Trafalgar' boats, through the 'Swiftsure' and 'Churchill' Classes to the older 'Valiant' submarines. For many years, the Royal Navy has given priority to the construction and manning of these vessels,

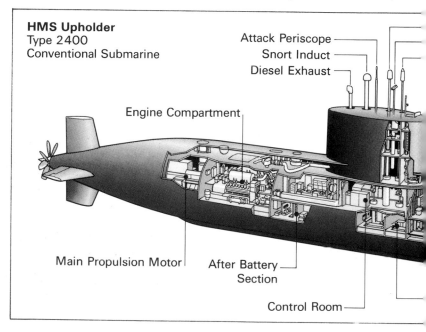

**HMS Upholder**
Type 2400
Conventional Submarine

Attack Periscope
Snort Induct
Diesel Exhaust
Engine Compartment
Main Propulsion Motor
After Battery Section
Control Room

although there are signs that the proposed prolonged building programme will not continue as costs increase. Recent reports indicate that a post-'Trafalgar' Class is being studied by the Ministry of Defence and a defence contractor.

The ballistic missile carrying submarine (SSBN) programme is directly linked to the politics of the Polaris replacement with the American Trident 2 missile. In 1987, Trident was expected to replace Polaris in the mid 1990s and the first 'Vanguard' Class submarine was under construction at Vickers Shipbuilding and Engineering with orders for the other three to be placed by 1990. The present SSBNs in Royal Naval service are the four 'Resolution' Class boats built in the 1960s. Work has been under way since 1986 on the modernization of the Clyde Submarine Base.

In 1986, the first of a new class of conventionally-powered and armed submarine, the Type 2400, was launched. The £100 million submarine will be the first of a projected class of at least eight to replace the older 'Oberon' Class submarines which were completed in the early and mid 1960s. The new class is named after the first boat, *Upholder*.

*Repulse, one of the four submarines built to carry the Polaris strategic deterrent. These submarines are based at Faslane in Scotland and one is always on patrol (RN/ Neptune).*

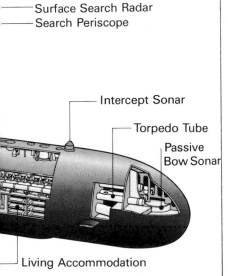

Esm Mast
Surface Search Radar
Search Periscope

Intercept Sonar

Torpedo Tube

Passive Bow Sonar

Living Accommodation

The role of the conventional patrol submarine includes anti-shipping operations in the North Sea and English Channel as well as oceanic task group operations — it is known that an 'Oberon' submarine was able to shadow Argentine submarines off that country's coastline in 1982. Other duties include mine warfare and operating with the Royal Marines.

## LIGHT AIRCRAFT CARRIERS

| Name | Pennant number | Flt Deck Code | Commissioned |
|------|----------------|---------------|--------------|
| 'INVINCIBLE' CLASS | | | |
| Invincible | R07 | N | 11 July 1980 |
| Illustrious | R06 | L | 21 June 1982 |
| Ark Royal | R07 | R | 1 November 1985 |

In 1980, the Royal Navy commissioned *Invincible*, the first of three light aircraft carriers which seem to have remained in the Navy Vote through the dark days of the late 1960s and early 1970s, disguised as 'Through Deck Cruisers'. The original role for these, the largest warships to be built in Britain for the Royal Navy since the Second World War, was to take a squadron of medium-range anti-submarine warfare helicopters to sea. Before the first ship was completed, however, the role was amended to include provision for a small squadron of Sea Harrier naval fighters. In addition, the ships have been very well fitted with naval communications equipment to act as task force command ship in any future conflict and as the flagship for the NATO Commander of Anti-Submarine Warfare Group 2 in the Atlantic.

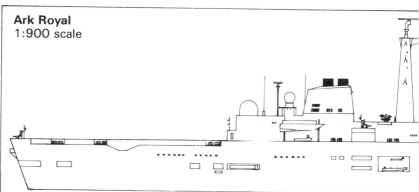

**Ark Royal**
1:900 scale

*Illustrious carries a powerful combination of search and missile radars for surveillance and self-defence purposes. Radar technology is now linked to powerful, very high capacity computers and other software-driven systems.*

There has been continued speculation that one of the three ships will be sold to a foreign buyer because the Royal Navy does not have the resources to man and operate the ship in peacetime. Just before the Falklands conflict in 1982, the Australian government expressed an interest in buying *Invincible* and in 1986 the Indian government made an apparent approach to acquire *Ark Royal*, settling instead for *Hermes*.

It is certainly true that the Royal Navy is only able to provide

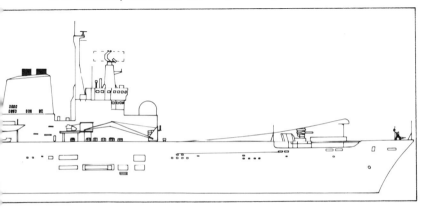

ships' companies for two carriers at one time and that there are only two front-line air groups of Sea Harrier and Sea King available to embark. In wartime, it is possible that a third air group could be made up from training units at Culdrose and Yeovilton. It is thus unlikely that the Royal Navy will consider a replacement class until well into the next century.

## ASSAULT SHIPS

| Name | Pennant number | Flt Deck Code | Commissioned |
|------|---------------|---------------|--------------|
| *Fearless* | L10 | FS | 25 November 1965 |
| *Intrepid* | L11 | ID | 11 March 1967 |

During the early 1980s there was considerable concern that the Royal Marines and NATO forces in the amphibious role would be without adequate sea-lift capability when the two British assault ships (LPDs), *Fearless* and *Intrepid*, were paid off at the end of the decade. If they were not replaced, considerable doubt would be placed on the future of the Royal Marines.

In 1986, the British government announced that it would be considering various options for replacing or renewing the existing

*In November 1986, the British Government confirmed its intention to continue operating* Fearless *and* Intrepid *into the mid 1990s to support the British commitment to NATO's Northern Flank. The Assault Ships, or LPDs to NATO, have a dock at the stern and a flight deck above. In this picture, Sea King HC4 and Gazelle AH1 helicopters are embarked on* Intrepid *(Patrick Allen).*

hulls, bearing in mind the role played by the ships in the Falklands and their recent excellent performance in Norwegian winter exercises. For normal peacetime operations, one is kept in refit/ reserve and the other is active.

The two existing assault ships, whilst having good communications, vehicle and personnel accommodation, need better helicopter facilities because this is the preferred way to travel ashore and to re-supply troops on the ground. In winter Norway, where the United Kingdom has a major reinforcement role, helicopters are vital to movement and re-supply of troops, but neither *Fearless* nor *Intrepid* has hangar facilities and the flight deck is really an open-air vehicle park. Interestingly enough, Sea Harriers were able to refuel aboard the assault ships during the first days in San Carlos Water during the Falklands campaign.

In peacetime, the assault ships have been used in the role of Dartmouth Training Ship, taking cadets and midshipmen to sea as part of their officer or non-commisioned officer training programmes.

# GUIDED MISSILE DESTROYERS

| Name | Pennant number | Flt Deck Code | Commissioned |
|------|----------------|---------------|--------------|
| 'TYPE' 82 | | | |
| *Bristol* | D23 | BS | 31 March 1973 |
| 'TYPE' 42 | | | |
| *Birmingham* | D86 | BM | 3 December 1976 |
| *Glasgow* | D88 | GW | 24 May 1977 |
| *Newcastle* | D87 | NC | 23 March 1978 |
| *Cardiff* | D108 | CF | 24 September 1979 |
| *Exeter* | D89 | EX | 19 September 1980 |
| *Southampton* | D90 | SN | 31 October 1981 |
| *Nottingham* | D91 | NM | 8 April 1983 |
| *Liverpool* | D92 | LP | 9 July 1982 |
| *Manchester* | D95 | MC | 16 December 1982 |
| *Gloucester* | D96 | GC | 11 September 1985 |
| *Edinburgh* | D97 | ED | 17 December 1985 |
| *York* | D98 | YK | 9 August 1985 |

Today's guided missile destroyers (DLG or DDH), of which two types are at sea, are the size of Second World War light cruisers and often have a similar role.

In the 1960s, when the CVA-01 aircraft carrier programme was cancelled, the Royal Navy was about to take delivery of the first

*Bristol was refitted in 1986 for Command & Control tasks but assumed the role of the Dartmouth Training Ship in 1987. She is the only example of a Type 82 guided missile destroyer designed to escort a new class of British aircraft carrier which was scrapped in 1966 (Robin Walker).*

Type 82 destroyer, armed with the Sea Dart area air defence missile and the Ikara anti-submarine warfare system. *Bristol*, the lead ship, was the only Type 82 completed and has since been modified for a command ship role; she has also recently been further refitted, with the Ikara removed and the new command, control, communications and intelligence (C³I) equipment installed. In August 1987, *Bristol* became the leader of the first Dartmouth Training Squadron for 15 years and was joined by the frigates *Rothesay* (due to pay off in 1988) and *Euryalus*.

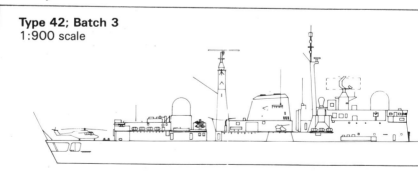

**Type 42; Batch 3**
1:900 scale

**Top** As built, the Type 42 area air defence destroyers were armed with limited close-in weapons, but as a result of the Falklands and Gulf conflicts, these weapons have been upgraded. This is Birmingham, as built (RN/Osprey).

**Above** Edinburgh is one of the final batch of Type 42 guided missile destroyers, optimized for area air defence, but also carrying anti-submarine weapons such as the Lynx helicopter (Robin Walker).

Twelve Type 42 destroyers are now in service as area defence ships, replacing the 'County' Class guided missile destroyers since the mid 1970s. They have the additional ability to engage in surface action with the Vickers Mk 8 gun and the embarked Lynx helicopter armed with the British Aerospace Sea Skua anti-shipping missile.

Two Type 42 destroyers were lost in the Falklands campaign. There has been criticism of the ships' close-in defence systems which meant that when engaged on radar picket duties, the destroyers had to be protected by a 'goalkeeper' Type 22 frigate, armed with the British Aerospace Sea Wolf point defence missile. Criticism has also been levelled at the lack of electronic warfare equipment in a Type 42, considering its area air defence role when on station as an exposed radar picket, some miles from the rest of the task group.

# FRIGATES

| Name | Pennant number | Flt Deck Code | Commissioned |
|---|---|---|---|
| TYPE 21 | | | |
| Amazon | F169 | AZ | 11 May 1974 |
| Ambuscade | F172 | AB | 5 September 1975 |
| Arrow | F173 | AW | 29 July 1976 |
| Active | F171 | AV | 17 June 1977 |
| Alacrity | F174 | AL | 2 July 1977 |
| Avenger | F185 | AG | 4 May 1978 |
| TYPE 22 (BATCH 1) | | | |
| Broadsword | F88 | BW | 4 May 1979 |
| Battleaxe | F89 | BX | 28 March 1980 |
| Brilliant | F90 | BT | 15 May 1981 |
| Brazen | F91 | BZ | July 1982 |
| TYPE 22 (BATCH 2) | | | |
| Boxer | F92 | XB | 22 December 1983 |
| Beaver | F93 | VB | 13 December 1984 |
| Brave | F94 | BA | August 1986 |
| London | F95 | LO | 5 June 1987 |
| Sheffield | F96 | SH | 1988 |
| Coventry | F98 | CV | 1988 |
| TYPE 22 (BATCH 3) | | | |
| Cornwall | F99 | CW | 1988 |
| Cumberland | F85 | CD | 1988 |
| Campbeltown | F87 | CN | 1990 |
| Chatham | F86 | CT | 1989 |

| Name | Pennant number | Flt Deck Code | Commissioned |
|------|---------------|---------------|--------------|
| **TYPE 23** | | | |
| *Norfolk* | F230 | NF | 1989 |
| *Marlborough* | | | 1990 |
| *Argyll* | | | 1990 |
| *Lancaster* | | | 1991 |
| **'LEANDER' CLASS (BATCH 1)** | | | |
| *Euryalus* | F15 | EU | 16 September 1964 |
| *Arethusa* | F38 | AR | 24 November 1965 |
| **'LEANDER' CLASS (BATCH 2)** | | | |
| *Minerva* | F45 | MV | 14 May 1966 |
| *Danae* | F47 | DN | 7 September 1967 |
| *Penelope* | F127 | PE | 31 October 1963 |
| *Juno* | F52 | JO | 17 August 1967 |
| **'LEANDER' CLASS (BATCH 2, TA)** | | | |
| *Cleopatra* | F28 | CP | 1 March 1966 |
| *Sirius* | F40 | SS | 15 June 1966 |
| *Phoebe* | F42 | PB | 14 April 1966 |
| *Argonaut* | F56 | AT | 17 August 1966 |
| **'LEANDER' CLASS (BATCH 3, GUN)** | | | |
| *Achilles* | F12 | AC | 9 July 1970 |
| *Diomede* | F16 | DM | 2 April 1971 |
| *Apollo* | F70 | AP | 28 May 1972 |
| *Ariadne* | F72 | AE | 10 February 1973 |
| **'LEANDER' CLASS (BATCH 3, SEAWOLF)** | | | |
| *Andromeda* | F57 | AM | 2 December 1968 |
| *Hermione* | F58 | HM | 11 July 1969 |
| *Jupiter* | F60 | JP | 9 August 1960 |
| *Scylla* | F71 | SC | 14 February 1970 |
| *Charybdis* | F75 | CS | 2 June 1972 |
| **TYPE 12 MODIFIED** | | | |
| *Rothesay* | F107 | RO | 23 April 1960 |
| *Plymouth* | F126 | PL | 11 May 1961 |

The role of the frigate has broadened since the Second World War when they were virtually just poorly armed, fast anti-submarine chasers. The modern frigates of the 'Broadsword' Class are well equipped with the most modern weapons and sensors. The Type 22s, in three Batches (with the latest returning to a conventional gun armament as well as carrying the latest surface-to-surface guided weapons), are the most modern frigates in the Royal Navy and it is planned that twelve will be in commission by 1990.

In addition, the modern Royal Navy has six 'Amazon' Class or

**Below** *Moving through the English Channel with a Lynx at alert, this Type 21 frigate, Ambuscade, was the last to be fitted with the Exocet missile system, installed for'ard of the bridge* (Robin Walker).

**Leander Class; Batch 2 (Towed Array)**
1:900 scale

**Bottom** *Beaver is one of the Type 22 frigates with a close-in air defence and anti-submarine role. She was the first of the Type to be complemented by two Lynx helicopters* (Robin Walker).

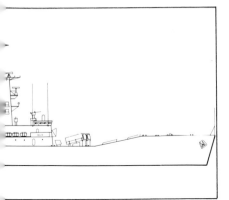

Type 21 frigates which are armed with the Vickers Mk 8 gun and Exocet missiles, as well as a Lynx helicopter. These privately-designed warships were commissioned in the mid 1970s and two were lost during the Falklands campaign when some anxiety was expressed about the design and construction of the super-structure. Again, these ships suffered from a lack of defensive armament.

Backing up these modern Types are the older, well-proven general purpose frigates of the 'Leander' Class which have been increasingly modified over the years and which now fall into five sub-classes, depending on their weapon and sensor fits : Batch 1 (Ikara), Batch 2 (Towed Array), Batch 2 (Exocet/Seacat), Batch 3 (Gun) and Batch 3 (Exocet/Sea Wolf). Two older Modified Type 12 frigates remain in commission as well, although they will be paid off by late 1988 when newer Type 22s come into service.

In the late 1980s and early 1990s, the Royal Navy will commission a new and highly versatile class of frigates, known as the Type 23 or

*A new generation of frigate will be commissioned during the next few years. The Type 23 is a powerful and useful addition to the Fleet, taking in many lessons from the Falklands.*

'Duke' Class. These will finally replace the older ships of the Fleet, with a primary role of using towed array sonar and an embarked EH 101 helicopter (from 1991) for anti-submarine warfare. Their secondary role will be participation in Surface Action Groups, armed with the Vickers Mk 8 gun and the American-designed Harpoon missile. The 'Duke' Class takes full account of the lessons learned in the Falklands conflict about damage control.

## OFFSHORE PATROL VESSELS

| Name | Pennant number | Flt Deck Code | Commissioned |
|------|--------|--------|--------------|
| 'CASTLE' CLASS | | | |
| Leeds Castle | P258 | LC | 25 August 1981 |
| Dumbarton Castle | P265 | DC | 26 March 1982 |
| 'ISLAND' CLASS | | | |
| Jersey | P295 | – | 15 October 1976 |
| Orkney | P299 | – | 25 February 1977 |
| Shetland | P298 | – | 14 July 1977 |
| Guernsey | P297 | – | 28 October 1977 |
| Lindisfarne | P300 | – | 3 March 1978 |
| Anglesey | P277 | – | 1 June 1979 |
| Alderney | P278 | – | 6 October 1979 |
| 'BIRD' CLASS (NI) | | | |
| Kingfisher | P260 | – | 8 October 1975 |
| Cygnet | P261 | – | 1976 |

| Name | Pennant number | Flt Deck Code | Commissioned |
|---|---|---|---|
| **'BIRD' CLASS (TRAINING)** | | | |
| *Peterel* | P262 | – | 7 February 1977 |
| *Sandpiper* | P263 | – | 16 September 1977 |
| *Redpoll* | P259 | – | March 1985 |
| **'PEACOCK' CLASS (HK)** | | | |
| *Peacock* | P239 | – | 14 July 1984 |
| *Plover* | P240 | – | 20 July 1984 |
| *Starling* | P241 | – | 7 August 1984 |
| *Swallow* | P242 | – | 16 November 1984 |
| *Swift* | P243 | – | 3 May 1985 |
| **'PROTECTOR' CLASS (FI)** | | | |
| *Protector* | P244 | – | 21 October 1983 |
| *Guardian* | P245 | – | 21 October 1983 |
| **'SENTINEL' CLASS** | | | |
| *Sentinel* | P246 | – | 14 January 1984 |
| **ICE PATROL** | | | |
| *Endurance* | A171 | ED | 1968 |

The Royal Navy is entrusted with the patrol of British economic and political interests in the North Sea, English Channel, South-West Approaches, Irish Sea and North Atlantic. To fulfil this demanding task, there are two classes of Offshore Patrol Vessels, backed up by the deployment of frigates and mines countermeasures vessels. In December 1986, the appointment of a Commodore Minor War Vessels and Mine Warfare (upgrading the command from that of

*Britain defends its economic interests, such as fishing and oil platforms, in a number of ways, including the use of 'Island' Class offshore patrol vessels. This is Guernsey, wearing the pennant (on her funnel) of the Fishery Protection Squadron and her international identification flags for entering Portsmouth Harbour (Robin Walker).*

*The Hong Kong Squadron of 'Peacock' Class offshore patrol vessels during so-called 'officer-of-the-watch manoeuvres'. 'Peacocks' are armed with the 76 mm OTO Melara gun and capable of self deployment to Australia (JSPRS).*

four-ringed Captain RN) demonstrated the importance of this area of activity for the modern Royal Navy.

Having served in the Falklands for special duties as despatch boats, the two 'Castle' Class OPVs now operate with the seven 'Island' Class craft to patrol Britain's offshore oil and gas installations and fishing grounds, and in an anti-terrorist role.

Closer inshore, especially around the coast of Northern Ireland, there are the two 'Bird' Class craft (the other two in the class being used for training Dartmouth cadets) and a planned class of 15 coastal training craft which will have a special patrol role, especially in wartime when they will be manned by the Royal Naval Reserve.

Overseas, the waters around the British colony of Hong Kong are patrolled by a new squadron of five 'Peacock' Class patrol vessels which were partly funded by the Hong Kong Government to assist the Royal Hong Kong Police with anti-terrorist, disaster relief, offshore patrol and search and rescue tasks.

Around the Falkland Islands, any would-be aggressors will be confronted by the two FI Patrol Vessels which were converted after the 1982 conflict from North Sea supply craft. Further south, the Ice Patrol Ship *Endurance* operates on a seasonal basis, looking after British interests as far south as Antarctica.

# MINES COUNTERMEASURES

| Name | Pennant number | Commissioned |
|------|---------|--------------|
| 'HUNT' CLASS | | |
| Brecon | M29 | 21 March 1980 |
| Ledbury | M30 | 11 June 1981 |
| Cattistock | M31 | 16 July 1982 |
| Cottesmore | M32 | 24 June 1983 |
| Brocklesby | M33 | 3 February 1983 |
| Middleton | M34 | 15 August 1984 |
| Dulverton | M35 | 3 November 1983 |
| Bicester | M36 | 14 February 1986 |
| Chiddingfold | M37 | 10 August 1986 |
| Atherstone | M38 | 30 January 1987 |
| Hurworth | M39 | June 1985 |
| Berkeley | M40 | November 1987 |
| Quorn | M41 | January 1988 |
| 'TON' CLASS (MH) | | |
| Bronington | M1115 | 4 June 1954 |
| Hubberston | M1147 | 14 October 1955 |
| Brereton | M1113 | 9 July 1954 |
| Iveston | M1151 | 29 June 1955 |
| Brinton | M1114 | 4 March 1954 |
| Kedleston | M1153 | 2 July 1955 |
| Kellington | M1154 | 4 November 1955 |
| Nurton | M1166 | 21 August 1957 |
| Sheraton | M1181 | 24 August 1956 |
| Maxton | M1165 | 19 February 1957 |
| 'TON' CLASS (CMS) | | |
| Cuxton | M1125 | 1953 |
| Upton | M1187 | 24 July 1956 |
| Soberton | M1200 | 17 September 1957 |
| Wotton | M1195 | 13 June 1957 |
| Glasserton | M1141 | 31 December 1954 |
| Wilton | M1116 | 14 July 1973 |
| 'RIVER' CLASS (CMS) | | |
| Waveney | M2003 | 12 July 1984 |
| Carron | M2004 | 29 September 1984 |
| Dovey | M2005 | December 1984 |
| Helford | M2006 | May 1985 |
| Humber | M2007 | May 1985 |
| Blackwater | M2008 | 14 June 1985 |
| Itchen | M2009 | September 1985 |
| Helmsdale | M2010 | 1986 |

| Name | Pennant number | Flt Deck Code | Commissioned |
|------|---------------|---------------|--------------|
| 'RIVER' CLASS (CMS) | | | |
| Orwell | M2011 | | 1986 |
| Ribble | M2012 | | 1986 |
| Spey | M2013 | | 1986 |
| Arun | M2014 | | 1986 |
| 'RACEHORSE' CLASS | | | |
| Sandown | M231 | | 1988 |
| + 11 | | | |

The threat posed by the silent underwater mine is great. In the 1960s and 1970s, it seemed that NATO, and the Royal Navy in particular, had all but ignored that threat. However, in recent years considerable emphasis has been placed on reforming the Royal Navy's mine warfare capability with the commissioning of the 'Hunt' Class of highly effective MCMVs together with the new 'River' Class which has totally replaced the 'Ton' Class minesweepers and minehunters manned by the Royal Naval Reserve.

There are still a number of 'Ton' Class minesweepers and minehunters available to support coastal operations, using conventional sweeping gear — towed mechanical cutters and acoustic or magnetic simulators — and equipment for what is termed mine-hunting, using unmanned submersible vehicles for checking suspicious objects on the seabed which have been detected by high

*Part of the strengthening of the NATO mine warfare defences was the commissioning of the 'Hunt' Class MCMVs, such as* Middleton, *seen here leaving Portsmouth Harbour* (Robin Walker).

definition sonar. Alternatively, a specially-trained clearance diver is sent down to disarm and recover the mine for intelligence purposes.

The Royal Navy has also ordered a new class of single-role minehunters, to be known as the 'Sandown' or 'Racecourse' Class. These craft are built of non-magnetic substances, including glass reinforced plastic, in the use of which Britain is a world leader.

# SUPPORT SHIPS

| Name | Pennant number | Flt Deck Code | Commissioned |
|------|---------|---------|--------------|
| 'ABDIEL' CLASS MINES COUNTERMEASURES SUPPORT SHIP | | | |
| Abdiel | N21 | – | 17 October 1967 |
| SEABED OPERATIONS VESSEL | | | |
| Challenger | K07 | CH | 20 August 1984 |

There are also two types of support ship which fly the White Ensign and are therefore classed as warships rather than the merchant-registered Royal Fleet Auxiliaries. These supports ships are *Abdiel*, the mines countermeasures support ship, and *Challenger*, the new and controversial seabed operations craft. *Abdiel* is due to pay off in 1988.

The Seabed Support Ship *Seaforth Clansman* is technically a chartered merchant ship, rather in the same way that ships are

*Challenger is one of the large warships in the Royal Navy but has been built for seabed operations, particularly diving, and carries specialist equipment for that task (Robin Walker).*

occasionally taken up from trade for supporting naval exercises such as the Falklands operations. It is thought that more chartered ships will be used to support the survey ship operations of the modern Royal Navy as the larger ocean-going ships are paid off for sale abroad.

From time to time, other vessels are chartered for specialist support roles, but they normally fly the RFA flag to allow them to operate in and out of commercial ports for re-supply and other non-combat tasks.

## SURVEY SHIPS

| Name | Pennant number | Flt Deck Code | Commissioned |
|------|----------------|---------------|--------------|
| **OCEAN SURVEY SHIPS** | | | |
| 'HECLA' CLASS | | | |
| Hecla | A133 | HL | 9 September 1965 |
| Hecate | A137 | HT | 20 December 1965 |
| 'IMPROVED HECLA' | | | |
| Herald | A138 | HE | 22 November 1974 |
| **COASTAL SURVEY SHIPS** | | | |
| 'BULLDOG' CLASS | | | |
| Bulldog | A317 | – | 21 March 1968 |
| Beagle | A319 | – | 9 May 1968 |
| Fox | A320 | – | 11 July 1968 |
| Fawn | A325 | – | 4 October 1968 |
| Roebuck | A130 | – | 2 October 1986 |
| **INSHORE SURVEY CRAFT** | | | |
| 'GLEANER' CLASS | | | |
| Gleaner | A86 | – | 5 December 1983 |

## COASTAL CRAFT

| Name | Pennant number | Commissioned |
|------|----------------|--------------|
| 'TRACKER' CLASS | | |
| Attacker | P281 | 11 March 1983 |
| Chaser | P282 | 11 March 1983 |
| Fencer | P283 | 21 March 1983 |
| Hunter | P284 | 21 March 1983 |
| Striker | P285 | 21 March 1983 |

**Above** *At the Royal Naval Air Station Culdrose in Cornwall, a maintainer from 849 Naval Air Squadron works on the Rolls-Royce Gnome engines of this Sea King AEW 2 airborne early warning helicopter. The Sea King, normally embarked in an 'Invincible' Class carrier, uses the Thorn EMI Electronics Searchwater radar to control Sea Harrier interceptions and to guard against sea-skimming missile attack (Rolls-Royce).*

**Below** *A Westland Lynx HAS 2 carrying four British Aerospace Sea Skua missiles during trials in 1983; the missile was employed in the Falklands conflict prior to actually entering operational service and is said to have been 100 per cent successful (Westland).*

**Above** HMS Fearless, one of two Assault Ships, is due to be replaced or modernized soon. Otherwise, the Royal Marines will have very little naval transport available to them. Note the ship's deck letters, FS, on the flight deck aft (PEB).

**Above right** Garage parking! The Devonport Dockyard frigate 'garage' for the refitting of the Royal Navy's escort fleet is one of the more important support features available to the Fleet today. The management of the Dockyard is now in private hands but must maintain the same service to the Royal Navy.

**Right** Warships are assisted in berthing and mooring by vessels of the Royal Maritime Auxiliary Service, a civilian-manned organization under the direction of the Ministry of Defence. This is the 'Felicity' Class single unit tractor tug, RMAS Genevieve (PEB).

**Below right** The Royal Marines can travel and be re-supplied in the field by the Royal Navy Support Helicopter force of 845 and 846 Naval Air Squadrons operating the Westland Sea King HC 4 (PEB).

**Below** HMS Battleaxe, providing point defence for the aircraft carrier HMS Ark Royal, comes alongside to refuel during exercises in the English Channel. Battleaxe, a Type 22 frigate, is equipped with the British Aerospace Sea Wolf missile system and two Westland Lynx HAS 2/3 helicopters armed with the Sea Skua anti-shipping missile (PEB).

**Above** Two WRNS (Women's Royal Naval Service) Engineer Officers working in a laboratory and tasked with investigations into the corrosion of gas turbine blades. The WRNS now trains for a series of jobs which keep pace with the developing technology of the modern Royal Navy (COI).

**Below** Queen Alexandra's Royal Naval Nursing Service, open to male and female nurses, serves the Fleet at the hospitals at Haslar (Portsmouth), Stonehouse (Plymouth) and Gibraltar. In addition, there is support from the Royal Naval Medical Service which provides technicians and medical assistants, as well as doctors and dentists (COI).

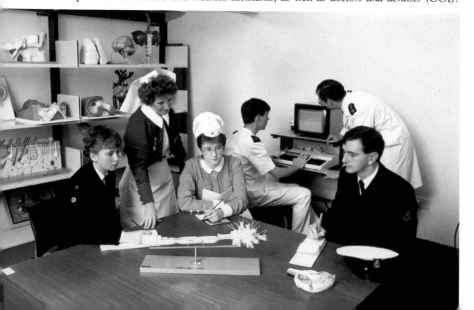

| Name | Pennant number | Commissioned |
|---|---|---|
| 'ARCHER' CLASS | | |
| Archer | P264 | 9 August 1985 |
| + 9 | | |

Delivery of this Class has been delayed by the builder's closure.

The British Admiralty Charts are highly regarded around the world. With the coming of the nuclear-powered deep-diving submarines, especially those carrying ballistic missiles, the need for such excellent and accurate charts of the seabed, and information about hydrothermal and saline layers, has become even greater.

*The production of charts and the provision of oceanographic data is an important part of the back-up service to the combat element of the modern Royal Navy; it is provided by survey ships like this 'Hecla' Class ocean-going type* (RN/Fleet Photographic Unit).

The Royal Navy operates a contracting fleet of three (soon to be two) ocean-going survey ships, supported by five coastal types and an inshore craft, *Gleaner*, which undertakes harbour and harbour approach work.

Admiralty Charts are prepared at Taunton and sold freely around the world, although much of the oceanographic information is classified and used for anti-submarine warfare planning and training. Every naval ship is equipped to carry out certain specialist oceanographic or meteorological tasks and some ships, especially the aircraft carriers, have a staff of weather and sea conditions forecasters embarked.

## THE ROYAL YACHT

*Britannia* (Pennant number A00, commissioned 14 January 1954) was very much in the news during 1986 when, during a voyage to meet HM The Queen and members of the Royal Family in the South Pacific, she rescued British and other nationals from strife-torn Aden. The Royal Yacht is used primarily for state and ceremonial occasions, but has a NATO war role as a hospital ship (much of which was practised during the Aden evacuation). The Royal Yacht is crewed by specially selected volunteers.

*Britannia leaves Portsmouth. The Royal Yacht is an important part of the Royal Navy's heritage and international prestige. She also has her uses, for example rescuing civilians stranded in Aden during a civil war in 1986 (RN/LA Photo Bob Dales).*

# WEAPONRY

## MISSILE SYSTEMS

During the Second World War, it became obvious that gun systems alone would not be capable of defending surface warships against aircraft. In the 1940s and 1950s research was undertaken by the United States, the Soviet Union, France and Britain which has resulted in these four countries leading the world in the development of guided weapon systems for naval use. These guided weapons fall into three areas : air-to-surface, surface-to-surface and sub-surface-to-surface.

The Royal Navy's first ventures into the guided missile field were the Shorts Seacat and Seaslug developments which came into service with the 'County' Class guided missile destroyers in the early 1960s. The Seacat has been updated since then and is still credible for certain threats, but the Seaslug is now out of service. During the 1970s, the threat from aircraft and air-launched sea-skimming missiles developed to a point where new systems had to be developed.

Destroyer-sized warships required a missile system with a true area defence capability to meet both the current threat of Mach 2 aircraft and missiles at sea level and the projected future threats of aircraft operating in an electronic warfare environment at stand-off ranges. Moreover, air-launched and sea-launched missiles have become faster, smaller and more agile as the missile manufacturers try to defeat the ship's defences.

The Royal Navy's answer to the area air defence threat is the Sea Dart, which first flew successfully with full guidance facilities operating in 1966. The missile equips the Type 82 and Type 42 destroyers, as well as being the only major shipboard defensive system of the 'Invincible' Class aircraft carriers which is capable of anything more than last-ditch defences.

Sea Dart was operational during the Falklands conflict, scoring seven confirmed kills of enemy aircraft. The tally might have been higher had the Argentine forces, having two Sea Dart systems in their own Type 42 destroyers, not been aware of the potential of the Sea Dart against targets in certain flight regimes — their attacking aircraft flew low to avoid the weapon. These low-level operations caused severe targeting and bomb-fuzing problems as well as bringing the aircraft into the missile engagement zones of the Seacat

and Sea Wolf systems, light guns and land-based weapons.

The Sea Wolf is a point defence weapon system which is fitted to the Type 22 frigates and certain of the 'Leander' Class frigates. It is very accurate and has been credited with the interception of over-the-horizon-launched sea-skimming missiles, multiple low-flying aircraft and even shells from the Vickers Mk 8 gun. It has been developed by British Aerospace, who have now developed the vertical launch version for future frigate classes including the Type

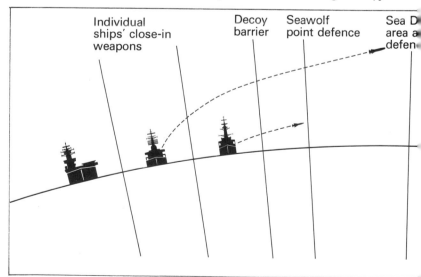

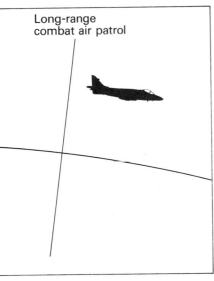

Long-range
combat air patrol

**Above left** *Sea Dart, carried adjacent to the ski-jump ramp in Illustrious, is the primary area air defence missile of the Royal Navy. Also shown in this picture is the Phalanx close-in defence system.*

**Left** *Air defence of the Fleet is provided in layers, by Sea Harriers, guided missiles and guns.*

**Above** *A new generation of warships will be protected by the short-range and highly effective vertical launch Seawolf system from British Aerospace. During 1986/87, trials were undertaken in a converted barge off South Wales before installation in the first Type 23 frigates (BAe).*

23. This system gives the advantage of multiple launches to defeat saturation attacks and does not require a launcher with a limited fire arc.

## SURFACE ACTION

In the 1970s, the gun armament of those destroyers and frigates allocated to the protection of task groups and convoys was

*A new generation of missile has entered service with the modern Royal Navy. It is the American-designed Harpoon surface-to-surface guided missile which can take a conventional warhead over the horizon. Type 22 Batch 3 and Type 23 frigates will receive the missile.*

considered to be inadequate for their defence against surface action from enemy missile-carrying craft. The British government therefore ordered the ship-launched Exocet missile from the French government to be retrofitted to the 'County' Class guided missile destroyers, certain Batch 2 and 3 'Leanders' and Type 21 frigates Later, the Batch 1 and 2 Type 22 frigates were also fitted with four Exocet launchers.

Exocet is effective over the horizon with guidance information fed into the system from helicopters or long-range maritime reconnaissance aircraft like the Nimrod. By 1990, the system will be obsolescent and will be replaced by the introduction of the American Harpoon system for the later Type 22 and the new Type 23 frigates. Batch 3 Type 22s were not designed as all-missile in the light of naval gunnery support experience from the Falklands, but were fitted with the Vickers Mk 8 gun. Batches 1 and 2 had been all-missile armed (except with the close-in Bofors 40mm/60 dual purpose gun) but *Broadsword* and *Brilliant* were obviously incapable of naval gunnery support tasks in the South Atlantic.

It is worth recording here that Sea Dart, Seacat and Sea Wolf have various degrees of anti-ship capability.

## SUBMARINES

Although the heavyweight torpedoes which arm the modern British submarines are wire-guided and accurate, the longer-range strike role requires the submarine-launched cruise-missile-type weapon, the McDonnell Douglas Sub-Harpoon. Like torpedoes, the encapsulated missile fits into the 533mm torpedo tubes of all British submarines, including the Polaris boats. After launching against a pre-determined threat, detected by sonar, the missile's own guidance system takes it to the target, with third-party in-flight guidance if necessary.

The United Kingdom's inventory of anti-ship and anti-submarine torpedoes still includes the Mk 8 developed in the Second World War, but is now mainly centered on the Mk 24 Tigerfish and the new Marconi Spearfish which commenced fleet weapons acceptance in 1988, prior to joining the Fleet. Attention is now turning to a new generation of submarine-launched weapons which would leave the water and fly unobserved to the enemy submarine contact before re-entering the sea and using an advanced seeker to hunt for their 'prey'. Helicopters and surface ships carry the lightweight Mk 46 or Stingray torpedoes for anti-submarine warfare. Frigates and other

**Above** *Stingray is the latest lightweight torpedo to join the inventory of the modern Royal Navy and can be dropped from ASW helicoptes or fired from special tubes for close-in anti-submarine defence of surface ships.*

**Below** *Designed to take an anti-submarine torpedo to attack an enemy submarine before it threatens the parent ship, the Ikara anti-submarine weapon carrier is fitted to a dwindling number of 'Leander' Class escorts. In Arethusa, the Ikara sysem replaced the 114 mm Mk 6 gun mounting* (Robin Walker).

warships use the Mk 32 shipborne torpedo weapons system to launch their torpedoes, whilst helicopters (and fixed-wing aircraft) drop their devices.

Surface warships which expect to see action against submarines — that is, frigates — were equipped in the early 1970s with the Anglo-Australian stand-off anti-submarine system Ikara. This is a guided weapon which is launched from a 'Leander' Class frigate to a point from which the torpedo which it carries can be dropped to attack a submarine detected by the ship's sonar.

## GUNNERY

Since the Second World War, gunnery in the Royal Navy has developed into computer-controlled precision weapons with unmanned turrets. The Vickers Mk 8 is the standard gun mounting for surface combat craft (frigates and destroyers), while the 'Peacock' Class offshore patrol craft which serve with the Hong Kong Patrol Squadron are armed with the Oto Melara 76mm dual purpose (anti-air and anti-surface) gun.

Close-in weapons include a variety of smaller calibre weapons,

*Standard gun armament for most surface combat ships, including the Type 42s, is the Vickers Mk 8 gun. Despite the open door, the mounting is fully automatic.*

*Royal Navy gunners from the Operations Branch train on a variety of weapons at Cambridge. Weapons in this picture include the Oerlikon twin 30 mm, single 20 mm (centre) and Bofors 40 mm mountings during a practice shoot against a towed target (Flight Refuelling).*

including the trusted Oerlikon 20 mm, the Bofors 40 mm and, since the Falklands campaign, the American Phalanx gatling gun (aircraft carriers and some Type 42s) and the Anglo-Dutch Goalkeeper system for Type 22 Batch 3 frigates and for refitted 'Invincible' Class aircraft carriers.

Submarines have not been armed with deck guns for some 20 years and it is not envisaged that they should engage in surface combat, unlike their predecessors. A true submarine will always fight below the waves.

Another type of defensive system is the active countermeasures launcher, carrying chaff (metal strips to confuse radar), metal smoke (to confuse electro-optical tracking systems) or flares (to decoy heat-seeking missiles). Computer control is used to fuze, arm and direct the decoy/countermeasures rockets, and so successful have the systems proved that Royal Fleet Auxiliaries are being equipped

*Electronic warfare systems have been greatly enhanced since the Falklands conflict, especially on the larger warships such as the 'Invincible' Class aircraft carriers.*

with them. They are of course purely defensive.

# WARSHIP SENSORS

Today, a modern warship is equipped with a variety of high-technology systems to assist in the detection of the enemy and in certain cases to assist in avoiding detection or defeating enemy action. Both surface ships and submarines use a wide selection of active (signal emitters) and passive (listening only) sensors above the waves (radio-based) or underwater (sound-based sonars).

Radar has been with the Royal Navy since just before the Second World War and it was developed throughout that conflict. All major warships carry radar for navigation, air and surface warning and for directing weapon systems. Very often a specific radar is used for a single important purpose, such as illuminating targets for the Sea Dart missile system.

Naval radar systems are becoming smaller with top weight

restriction (the size of the antenna) and because micro-processor techniques are being developed to increase the 'power' of the radar, assisting the operator to glean as much information as possible about the contact, distinguishing it from the background clutter of sea and sky.

Search radar is used to detect potential enemy attacks, and individual weapon systems illuminate the contact for possible attack. Most long-range radars are capable of identifying the contact by means of a coded transmission to which a friendly aircraft's transponder will automatically reply with the correct code. If the code is incorrect, the usual result is the launch of a missile.

The modern naval environment must be electronically 'quiet' because even a transmission of radio waves lasting only seconds can give away a ship's position and, by examination of the frequency and other electronic signatures, the enemy can determine its type and class. In certain respects, warship commanders are back to the days prior to radar, relying on the eyes of the ship's company. Modern

*The modern Royal Navy is a world leader in passive towed array sonar technology and now has systems in submarines and anti-submarines escorts like the frigate* Phoebe. *Towed arrays have an extremely wide range and were developed as a counter against the deep diving and fast new generation of Soviet submarines (Robin Walker).*

methods of warning are available to a task force, however, including airborne early warning from a Sea King helicopter, information from a radar picket or the use of electronic surveillance measures — the so-called passive electronic warfare. Most British surface combat craft (and soon all submarines) are fitted with ESM to detect the emissions of enemy warships and aircraft before their active radars are in range to detect the ESM-carrying ship. It is then possible to use the electronic intelligence data to pre-programme a long-range missile attack (a pre-emptive strike) or to determine the strength of any enemy force.

Although submarines are equipped with radar systems, the basic sensor used is sonar. Again, this comes in two forms: active and passive. Most submarine commanders, especially those in command of SSBNs, want to remain silent, listening to others. For attack with torpedoes or torpedo tube-launched missiles, the passive sonar can be used, but better attack data, including range, can be determined by using active sound-emitting sonar.

*Britain's new generation of anti-submarine helicopter will be the Anglo-Italian EH 101, a vital weapon in the fight against submarines and a partner with towed-array frigates in the ASW team. The first pre-production helicopter was rolled out at Yeovil in April 1987; note the development Sea King HC4 behind (Westland).*

*Modern command and control systems, such as the Ferranti CS 500, use the latest touch and graphics technology. This is the Ferranti bid for the Type 23 contract.*

Surface ships and Sea King helicopters carry active sonar for anti-submarine operations, but in this area too there is a move towards passive systems such as towed array which is currently being made available for frigates and submarines. This system is a long pipe with sound receivers especially calibrated to detect the slightest noise from a submarine, and because the array is long, there is less self-generated noise from the host warship to disturb the sonar. When a possible submarine is heard, an aircraft, usually a Sea King or (by the early 1990s) an EH 101, will be deployed to localize the contact and determine whether it is a submarine target.

As well as electronic warfare systems, modern warships are being equipped with powerful electro-optical sensors capable of night vision using thermal imaging modules, linked to low-light television and other vision aids.

Aboard modern warships computer technology has been harnessed to provide the central action data systems which calculate data for the weapons, sensors and navigational systems, including inertial navigation for the larger surface ships and all submarines. With almost instant read-outs, the commander in his below-decks operations room can make a decision which could help destroy an enemy or save the ship in combat.

Electronic control includes that for the fuel flow of modern gas turbine engines, many of which can be controlled from the bridge; such turbine-powered warships rarely have men permanently stationed in the engine rooms, and use the central control room principle. The same developments have been seen in the nuclear-powered submarine and will also eventually come about in the smaller warships.

# NAVAL AIR POWER

Founded before the First World War as the Royal Naval Air Service and surviving control by the Royal Air Force between 1918 and 1937, naval aviation in the United Kingdom is now known as the Fleet Air Arm. Through the offices of Flag Officer, Naval Air Command, naval helicopters and fixed-wing aircraft squadrons based at naval air stations provide the air assets to the Commander-in-Chief Fleet, through Flag Officer Third Flotilla.

The Fleet Air Arm's main role is to provide organic (contained within the force) air cover for naval operations, from a single helicopter in a small ship's flight to the two air groups of nine Sea King HAS 5s, three Sea King AEW 2s and five Sea Harrier FRS 1s in the 'Invincible' Class aircraft carriers, All of the air assets of the Fleet Air Arm are declared, earmarked or assigned to NATO, or could be made available to NATO operations should the need arise.

The 1987 'order of battle' was as follows:

| Aircraft | Squadrons | Station |
|---|---|---|
| **AIR DEFENCE AND STRIKE** | | |
| Sea Harrier FRS 1 | 800, 801 | 'Invincible' Class CVS |
| | 899 | Headquarters/training |
| Harrier T 4 (N) | 899 | Training |
| **ANTI-SUBMARINE WARFARE** | | |
| Sea King HAS 5 | 810, 819 | Shore-based |
| | 814, 820 | 'Invincible' Class CVS |
| | 824, 826 | RFA/Shore-based |
| | 706 | Training |
| Wasp HAS 1 | 829 | Type 12/'Leander' FFH |
| **ANTI-SUBMARINE/ANTI SURFACE VESSEL WARFARE** | | |
| Lynx HAS 2/3 | 815, 829 | FFH/DDH/Training |
| **AIRBORNE EARLY WARNING** | | |
| Sea King AEW 2 | 849A, 849B Flight | 'Invincible' Class |
| | 849 | Headquarters/training |
| **COMMANDO ASSAULT** | | |
| Sea King HC 4 | 845, 846 | Shore-based/LPD |
| Sea King HC 4 | 707 | Training |
| **AIRCREW TRAINING** | | |
| Lynx HAS 2/3 | 702 | Training |
| Gazelle HT 2 | 705 | Basic training |
| Jetstream T 2/3 | 750 | Observer training |

| Chipmunk T 10 | 771/BRNC Flight | Air experience |
|---|---|---|
| **FLEET SUPPORT and SAR** | | |
| Wessex HU 5 | 771, 772 | Shore-based |
| **FLEET REQUIREMENTS** | | |
| Canberra (various) | FRADU | Shore-based |
| Hunter (various) | FRADU | Shore-based |
| **SERVICE SUPPORT** | | |
| Sea Devon C 20 | Station flights | Shore-based |
| Sea Heron C 1 | Station flights | Shore-based |

# AIR DEFENCE AND STRIKE

Aboard the two light aircraft carriers of the 'Invincible' Class which are active at any one time — the third is in refit or reserve because there is not sufficient aircrew, maintainers nor ship's company to keep three at sea — a squadron of five British Aerospace Sea Harrier FRS 1s and eight pilots is embarked to provide both air defence for the task group and a strike capability, both nuclear and conventional.

*This Sea Harrier pilot, Lieutenant Alistair McLaren, joined the Royal Navy in 1978 and after training joined 809 squadron for Illustrious' Falkland Islands Patrol in 1982. Since then he has flown the famous aircraft with 801 Sqn (Invincible) and 800 Sqn (Illustrious). Since September 1986 he has been an Air Warfare Instructor with 899 Sqn at Yeovilton where he teaches pilots how to use the Sea Harrier in combat (RN).*

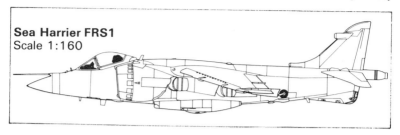

**Sea Harrier FRS1**
Scale 1:160

This ability was graphically demonstrated during Operation Corporate in 1982 when Sea Harriers from 800, 801 and 899 Squadrons from ship and land bases were highly successful against Argentine air attacks and, to a limited extent, in ground attack.

It is thought that a major threat to a naval task group would be Soviet long-range maritime reconnaissance aircraft which could guide submarine-launched cruise missiles against the surface ships. The Sea Harrier, aided by the organic Sea King AEW 2 helicopters equipped with the advanced Searchwater airborne early warning radar, is used to intercept such shadowing aircraft in an action known as 'hacking the shad'. Modern naval task groups operate a

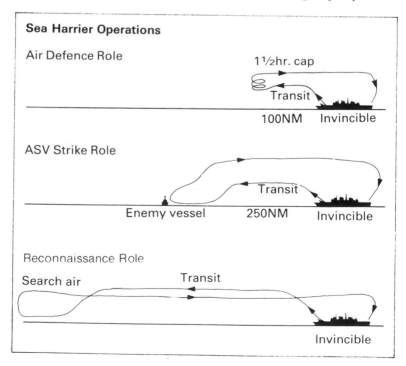

**Sea Harrier Operations**

Air Defence Role

1½hr. cap

Transit

100NM    Invincible

ASV Strike Role

Transit

Enemy vessel    250NM    Invincible

Reconnaissance Role

Search air        Transit

Invincible

*Sea Harrier FRS 1, the Fleet fighter of the 1980s and equipped for maritime strike, fighter and reconnaissance duties from 'Invincible' Class aircraft carriers (RN/ Heron).*

three-tier air defence environment — firstly the Sea Harrier screen, followed by the Sea Dart area air defence missile and finally the close-in defence of the Sea Skua/Seacat missiles and the Phalanx/ Goalkeeper gunnery systems.

In 1988, the Sea Harrier force will be equipped with the British Aerospace Sea Eagle anti-shipping missile for medium to long-range strikes against enemy shipping. This will complement the Lynx HAS 2/3 helicopters equipped with the Sea Skua missile which are operated by many frigates and destroyers.

The Sea Harrier will be modified from FRS 1 to FRS 2 standard to give the aircraft a more capable radar to detect and track low-flying targets against which a new generation of air defence missiles will be used, including replacements for the Sidewinder in both medium and short ranges. By 1988, a further nine Sea Harriers will be delivered to the Fleet Air Arm and in 1986 a new training programme began to qualify additional pilots to man these new aircraft.

**Sea King HAS 5**
Scale 1:160

# ANTI-SUBMARINE WARFARE

The Sea King helicopter, now in its Mk 5 variant, is the Royal Navy's principal airborne anti-submarine warfare system. It is equipped with Plessey's Type 195M dipping sonar to actively seek submarines, the Plessey/Dowty sonobuoy systems which are expandable listening devices, the MEL Sea Searcher tactical radar and the Racal Avionics Orange Crop electronic surveillance measures system to passively track enemy radar emissions. Some helicopters are equipped with the Texas Instrument's MAD (magnetic anomaly detector) which is capable of detecting small changes in the Earth's magnetic field which could indicate the presence of a submarine.

The Sea King HAS 6, an advanced sonar/sonics systems update, is planned to enter service from 1989, but at present there are 78 Sea King HAS 5s in service with six front-line squadrons and a training unit; a total of 116 Sea King airframes has been ordered from Westland over the last 15 years. The Sea King Mk 6 and the Lynx Mk 8 (in its secondary role of ASW) will complement the first of the advanced, three-engined Anglo-Italian EH 101 helicopters which are due to enter service after 1991.

It is now known that the Wasp will be phased out of service in 1988 when the last of the Type 12 frigates which are not Lynx-capable are paid off; already *Endurance*, Britain's only ice patrol ship, has been modified to take the Lynx and the last Ocean-type survey ship will also have been paid off, albeit prematurely, by 1988.

The Lynx, although it has replaced the Wasp in the Type 21 and 'Leander' Class frigates, where anti-submarine warfare has been the primary role, is now classed as an anti-submarine strike and surface search helicopter, with ASW as an important secondary role.

Lynx and Sea King helicopters are now receiving the advanced Stingray lightweight torpedo; 820 Squadron, embarked in the last of

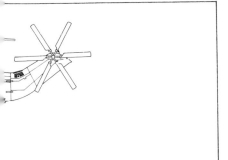

**Below** *Folded and positioned on the lift, one of 820 Squadron's Sea King HAS 5s is brought up to the flight deck of Illustrious during routine flying operations. The Sea King MK 5 is rated as the best medium ASW helicopter in the world and in June 1987 GEC Avionics received a contract to improve still further the helicopter's 'sonics' kit* (RN).

the three 'Invincible' Class light aircraft carriers, *Ark Royal*, is the first unit to be fully operational with the Marconi-built weapon.

# ANTI-SURFACE VESSEL WARFARE

Although the Wasp is capable of carrying the French-designed AS12 wire-guided anti-shipping missile, the Lynx and its British

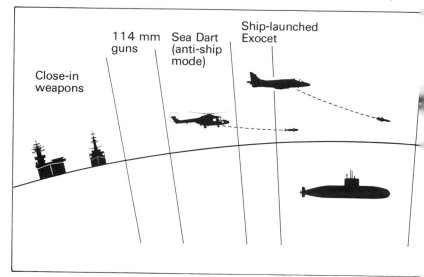

Aerospace Sea Skua system has brought the stand-off anti-surface vessel warfare capability of the Fleet Air Arm to state of the art. The missile system was tested operationally in the Falklands campaign even before it had officially entered service with the Royal Navy, and since then exercises have proved a number of tactics for the helicopter-missile combination.

In about 1990, the Lynx HAS 8 will enter service with a modified avionics suite which will include a 360 degrees radar interfaced with

Air-launched Sea Skua/Sea Eagle
-Submarine-launched weapons or
mid-course guided harpoon

**Left** *Surface action is layered in defence and attack. Air, surface and sub-surface systems are used.*

**Below left** *To enable the Lynx to operate in the perceived threat conditions of the 1990s, the Royal Navy intends to fit the helicopter with advanced systems, including a 360 degrees radar and passive night vision equipment. In this artist's impression, the helicopter is carrying two Sea Skua missiles and a Stingray torpedo (Westland).*

**Below** *In 1988, the Royal Navy is introducing the BAe Sea Eagle standoff anti-shipping missile to enhance the strike capability of the Sea Harrier force.*

the Sea Skua to allow the helicopter to engage a target and then turn away from the threat of anti-aircraft fire (including missiles) while still keeping the target and the missile illuminated by radar for targeting. In view of the increase in the surface search role, the Mk 8 will be fitted with the GEC Avionics Sea Owl passive identification system which allows the helicopter's observer to locate a target without the target being aware of his action.

It is not thought that there is a need for helicopters in Royal Naval

service to be equipped with the Sea Eagle system, about to come into service with the Sea Harrier force, although it has been specified for the Indian Navy.

Lynx small ship flights are currently embarked in Type 21 and 22 frigates, Type 42 destroyers and the 'Leander' Class towed array sonar frigates. There is a training and headquarters unit in Portland, the home base for the individual ship's flights, and it is with this Squadron that HRH The Duke of York is a helicopter warfare instructor.

# AIRBORNE EARLY WARNING

In 1978, when the last Gannet AEW 3 fixed-wing airborne early warning radar-carrying aircraft were paid off, the Royal Navy was left without any organic AEW coverage. When the Task Force sailed for the South Atlantic in April 1982, it was thus without AEW and the loss of the guided missile destroyer *Sheffield* graphically demonstrated this deficiency.

As a result of the conflict, Westland Helicopters and Thorn EMI Electronics combined the existing Sea King Mk 2 airframe with the highly reliable Searchwater radar to create the world's first operational AEW helicopter. The Royal Navy now has 849 Squadron in commission as the AEW helicopter flight attached to each aircraft carrier. Ten Sea King AEW 2 helicopter conversions have been funded, enough to provide two sea-going flights and a headquarters/ training unit at RNAS Culdrose, which will remain in commission for the foreseeable future.

## COMMANDO ASSAULT

The Sea King HC 4, one of the stars of the Falklands campaign, has now replaced the venerable Wessex HU 5 in service with the Fleet Air Arm's two front-line Commando Support squadrons, 845 and 846, both based at RNAS Yeovilton. Their role is to support the operations of the Royal Marines Commando forces ashore and afloat, with a primary responsibility for the NATO Northern Flank

**Left** *In the 1980s, the 'eyes' of the Fleet are the embarked flights of Sea King AEW 2 helicopters, carrying the Thorn EMI Electronics Searchwater radar to detect hostile sea-skimming missiles and attacking aircraft. The helicopters are flown by 849 Squadron (RN/Culdrose).*

**Right** *Sea King HC 4 helicopters are now the front line air commando support for the Royal Marines and are flown by 845 and 846 Squadrons based at Yeovilton. In winter, several flights deploy to Arctic Norway.*

in Norway, where training is carried out each winter season.

Also at Yeovilton is the RN Commando Helicopter support training unit, based on 707 Squadron, which is equipped with the Sea King HU 5.

## AIRCREW TRAINING

Elementary flying training for the Fleet Air Arm is undertaken by the Royal Air Force, following selection at Biggin Hill and/or air experience and grading with the Britannia Royal Naval College Flight, based at Roborough (Plymouth), not far from Dartmouth.

After attending this course on Bulldog aircraft, the future helicopter pilot will be posted to Culdrose and become a basic rotary-wing student with 705 Squadron flying the Gazelle HT 2 helicopter. This unit's instructors also provide the pilots for the Sharks helicopter display team.

After graduation from the wings course, the pilot is then streamed into anti-submarine warfare with 706 (medium) and 702 (light) Squadrons, or commando support with 707 Squadron. Operational ASW training for the Sea King HAS 5 is given by 810 Squadron and for Sea Harriers initially by the RAF at Wittering, the UK Harrier force headquarters, and then by 899 Squadron at Yeovilton; other streams use the operational squadrons.

Observers for the Sea King and Lynx fleets are trained at Culdrose, gaining flying experience with 750 Squadron's Jetstream

T 2 and T 3 aircraft (the latter having the Racal ASR 360 radar) before going to 702 (Lynx) or 810 (Sea King) Squadron.

## FLEET SUPPORT and SEARCH AND RESCUE

This sector of the Fleet Air Arm is the province of the Wessex, although only two second-line units remain as users of the helicopter which was once the mainstay of the commando support squadrons. These are 771 Squadron at Culdrose, which has an SAR function not only operationally but also for training, and 772 Squadron at Portland, which has a varied role supporting Royal Fleet Auxiliary replenishment ships, most of which are now helicopter-capable, providing the staff of Flag Officer Sea Training with logistical support and SAR at Portland and providing a detached flight at Lee-on-Solent.

**Above left** *Navigation training for helicopter observers is carried out in the BAe Jetstream. The observer is a vital link in the command chain, and his role includes actually fighting the helicopter and co-ordinating the maritime battle. Others are trained for airborne early warning (RN).*

**Right** *Close co-operation is maintained between the Royal Navy and the Royal National Lifeboat Institution, including frequent exercises such as this one off the Scottish coast with a Sea King from 819 Sqn (RN).*

# FLEET REQUIREMENTS

Operated by a commercial contractor, Flight Refuelling Limited, on behalf of the Royal Navy, the Fleet Requirements and Air Direction Unit at Yeovilton flies various marks of Hunter and Canberra jets. The pilots are civilians with considerable service experience in the RAF or Royal Navy and their job is to provide aircraft for radar calibration, to act as 'targets' and to be directed around the sky by ground-based fighter direction officers under training as well as by observers under training with 849 Squadron in the Sea King AEW 2.

Recently, the Hunters and Canberras have been supplemented by American-registered but French-built Falcon jets which simulate strike aircraft and which can carry electronic warfare equipment to train and test ships and aircraft of the Fleet. FRADU often provides the Blue Herons display team, the only civilian-manned military jet team in the world.

# SERVICE SUPPORT

Three de Havilland types, all of 1950s vintage, make up the small but hard-working service support force of the Royal Navy. There are

*FRADU operates a number of aircraft for the Fleet Air Arm, flown and maintained by civilian staff but based at Yeovilton. Aircraft such as the Hunter GA 11 are used.*

eight Sea Devon and Sea Heron communications aircraft, mainly based at Culdrose, as well as 16 Chipmunks, including those mentioned above with the BRNC Flight. Several of the Chipmunks are utilized at weekends for gliding and other air experience duties. When the 'Clipper' communications squadron at Lee-on-Solent was disbanded in 1981, part of the job passed to the RAF at Northolt, and two British Aerospace HS 125 executive transports were funded by the Royal Navy to be operated by the RAF for the provision of special communications facilities. In addition, the Sea Herons are still used in that role from Yeovilton.

## ROYAL NAVAL AIR STATIONS

Although the main operational role of the Fleet Air Arm is at sea, there is a considerable requirement for a good shore-based chain of establishments to back up the sea-going force. Aircraft are based ashore at Royal Naval Air Stations and are repaired, along with the helicopters of the other two services, at two Royal Naval Aircraft Repair yards.

There are four principal naval air stations in the United Kingdom and a smaller one is co-located with an international airport in Scotland. The four main air stations are positioned to support naval base and dockyard facilities along the English Channel.

Yeovilton in Somerset is the headquarters of the Fleet Air Arm and the naval air station is host to various lodger units, including the headquarters of the Flag Officer Naval Air Command, the Fleet Requirements and Air Direction Unit, the Fleet Air Arm Museum, the Air Direction School, 3 Commando Brigade Air Squadron Royal Marines and a Naval Aircraft Support Unit. Sea Harrier and Sea King HC 4 front-line units are deployed from Yeovilton and the station is also the home of the parallel training units.

On the Lizard Peninsula in Cornwall, Culdrose is the busiest helicopter airfield in Europe, supporting the main helicopter anti-submarine warfare effort and the newly-created helicopter airborne early warning squadron. In addition, the RAF's Sea King Training Unit is a lodger along with various Schools including that of aircraft handling. Besides the front-line Sea King units, Culdrose is host to the training units for basic flying training and observers. It is a major search and rescue centre for the south-west of England, the Irish Sea and the coast of Ireland.

Helicopters have been flying at Portland for more than 40 years and it is now the home of the small ship flights of Wasp and,

**Left** *One of the most famous helicopter pilots in the Royal Navy in recent years has been Lieutenant HRH The Prince Andrew, Duke of York. During the Falklands conflict, he was a pilot with 820 Squadron serving on* Illustrious, *and later trained on the Lynx HAS 2. He is pictured here at Portland in 1983 when still a Sub Lieutenant, wearing the aircrew coverall, green roll-neck shirt and white aircrew flying gloves (RN/Ken Rixon).*

**Below** *Culdrose's radar room provides air traffic and flight safety information for naval, military and civilian aircraft operating over the south-west of the United Kingdom. The controllers are all Sub Lieutenants in this picture, supervised by the watch commander, a Lieutenant Commander (RN/Culdrose).*

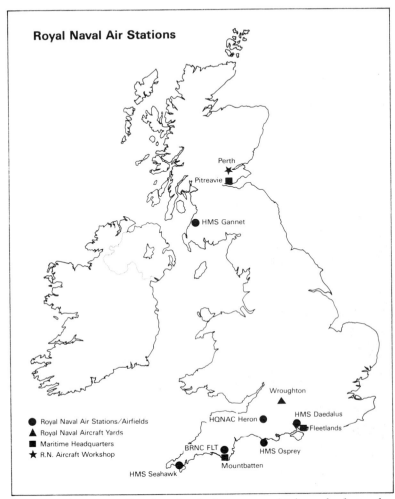

**Royal Naval Air Stations**

Perth
Pitreavie
HMS Gannet

Wroughton
HQNAC Heron
HMS Daedalus
Fleetlands
BRNC FLT
HMS Osprey
Mountbatten
HMS Seahawk

● Royal Naval Air Stations/Airfields
▲ Royal Naval Aircraft Yards
■ Maritime Headquarters
★ R.N. Aircraft Workshop

increasingly, Lynx. Besides the helicopters which embark in the frigates and destroyers of the Fleet, training and trials are carried out there. In addition, a squadron of Wessex HU 5 helicopters supports the requirements of the Flag Officer Sea Training and local search and rescue operations in this busy area of the English Channel.

Engineering and other specialist non-flying training is carried out at Lee-on-Solent, facing the Isle of Wight between Portsmouth and Southampton. This airfield is alongside the Solent and is connected to the water with a ramp which was used for naval hovercraft trials in the 1970s. Today, the only regular flying activity is that of the search and rescue flight equipped with Wessex HU 5 helicopters. Close by

Based at Lee-on-Solent, the rescue flight, known locally as 'Lee SAR' is primarily engaged in naval rescue but inevitably the majority of the peacetime tasks it is asked to perform are for civilians, and this service gives considerable job satisfaction for the aircrew. Lee SAR flies the Wessex HU 5 helicopter, here carrying out winching drills with a lifeboat (RN/Daedalus).

Lee-on-Solent is the British services' helicopter repair yard at Fleetlands, on the edge of Portsmouth Harbour.

In Scotland, the Sea King anti-submarine helicopter unit which protects the Clyde Submarine Base is lodged with the Scottish transatlantic airport at Prestwick on the Ayrshire coast. The resident units, 819 and 824 Squadrons, provide search and rescue cover for the Western Isles, the Northern Irish coast and the local mainland area. On the other side of the country near Perth is the long-term helicopter repair yard and stores centre.

All naval air stations have ships' names which at present are: Yeovilton, HMS *Heron*; Culdrose, HMS *Seahawk*; Portland, HMS *Osprey*; Lee-on-Solent, HMS *Daedalus*; and Prestwick, HMS *Gannet*.

# BY SEA, BY LAND – THE ROYAL MARINES

The Royal Marines are the Royal Navy's sea soldiers and, although they are organized along basically army lines, including ranks and operational equipment, they remain fully integrated with the Royal Navy. The Corps has a long and exciting history going back to the seventeenth century, although the image of the Royal Marine Commando has been created during the last quarter of a century. The modern Royal Marine has to be prepared to fight in tropical, arctic or temperate conditions, supporting the Royal Navy or on soldier-like peace-keeping operations in places such as Northern Ireland, Cyprus and Belize.

Today, the Royal Marines Commando Force is made up as follows:

**Headquarters** 3rd Commando Brigade Royal Marines

Operational units
40, 42 and 45 Commandos
29 Commando Regiment, Royal Artillery
59 Independent Commando Squadron, Royal Engineers
Commando Logistics Regiment

Commandant General Royal Marines
*Britain's sea soldiers are commanded by Lieutenant General Sir Martin Garrod KCB OBE, the most senior Royal Marine. General Garrod joined 40 Commando RM as a Rifle Troop Subaltern, serving in Malta and later Cyprus, Malaya and Northern Ireland, reflecting the peace-keeping and policing roles of the Royal Marines since the 1950s. In 1978 he assumed command of 40 Cdo and took his men to Northern Ireland as the first resident RM 'battalion'. Since then he has been Colonel Operations/Plans, Commander of 3 Cdo Brigade RM and Chief of Staff to CGRM. He was appointed CGRM in May 1987 (RM).*

3rd Commando Brigade Air Squadron
539 Assault Squadron
Special Boat Squadrons
Raiding Squadrons

In addition, there is a flourishing and important Royal Marines Reserve with supporting units based around the country.

## THE FIGHTING SOLDIER-SAILOR

In the second half of the 1980s, the Royal Marine Commando is a dedicated, efficient and formidable fighter. He is an infantryman with a number of specialist weapons and pieces of kit, especially for operations in Northern Norway, and the average RM Commando can carry enough ammunition, food and general equipment to fight and survive for at least a week in the freezing temperatures of the Arctic. His basic equipment is the new Enfield SA 80 automatic rifle and more than 60 lb of kit.

*Royal Marines training on Salisbury Plain. The weapons illustrated are the General Purpose Machine Gun (GPMG) and the Self-Loading Rifle (SLR), both standard infantry weapons.*

Training takes place at the Commando Training Centre at Lympstone in Devon, where both potential officer and marine are trained together, the only difference being that the officer candidate is required to complete the tasks more quickly; for example, he has to finish an endurance march some ten minutes earlier than a basic marine recruit.

To gain the coveted green beret, a Royal Marine has a 12-month course which is said to push the men to the very limits of their endurance in mental as well as physical terms; the modern Royal Marine is a thinking soldier and part of an elite. It is hard work and only one in two hundred can expect to pass.

During the year-long course, the Royal Marine recruit will have completed nearly two miles of obstacle course consisting of bog, mud and water-filled tunnel and run back to Lympstone in 70 minutes, completed a nine-mile run in 90 minutes with some 30 lb of equipment and completed a Dartmoor yomp of 30 miles in seven hours with 30 lb of equipment.

After Lympstone, operational training takes place at one of the Commando units and this can last as much as nine months. Marines have the opportunity to specialize as swimmer-canoeists, parachutists, helicopter aircrew, mountain and arctic warfare leaders and mortarmen, to name but a few. The men nonetheless remain proud of the fact that they are, despite the specializations of their careers, Royal Marines.

## COMMANDO UNITS

The main fighting arms of the 3rd Commando Brigade are the three Commando Units. These are 40 and 45, which are arctic warfare trained, and 42 which, although its men are capable of the arctic role, are trained for other areas. Each Commando has a total of between 900 and 1000 officers and men, with 45 Cdo having an extra company – Whiskey Company – of the Royal Netherlands Marine Corps under its command. All three Commando units have specialist troops or smaller formations of troops under their command, including commando-trained engineers and artillery. 45 Cdo Group is the only one with the suffix 'Group' because of its combination of specialist skills under one military formation.

40 Commando Royal Marines was formed at Deal in Kent in February 1942, taking part six months later in the Dieppe raid and later the invasion of Sicily, Italy and Yugoslavia. After the Second World War, 40 Cdo took part in internal security operations in

*In the Falklands, Commando helicopter support by the Royal Navy included the widespread use of the Sea King HC 4 helicopter, seen here working from a small light helicopter landing site at San Carlos Bay (UKLF).*

Palestine, Hong Kong, Malaya, the Suez Canal Zone, Cyprus, Borneo and Northern Ireland. In 198, it was the first unit of Royal Marines to land on the Falkland Islands during Operation Corporate, the liberation of the islands from Argentine control. Supporting the Welsh Guards after the tragedy at Bluff Cove, 40 Cdo then moved in support of them to Port Stanley as well as deploying to West Falkland to mop up the Argentine military operations there. Since the South Atlantic conflict, 40 Commando Royal Marines has completed its sixth operational tour in Northern Ireland and has also provided men for the United Nations peace-keeping force in Cyprus.

Dating back to 1943 and the reorganization of the British commando and Royal Marines forces, 42 Cdo was originally the 1st Battalion Royal Marines and as such had fought with valour and distinction from 1760, including periods in the American War of Independence, the Crimea and in China. During the Second World War, 42 Cdo was operational in India and Burma and it deployed to Malaya in 1950-52 during the Communist terrorist period. It then spent a time as a Malta-based unit before returning to the United Kingdom to act as a training unit.

With the advent of the Commando Carriers *Albion* and *Bulwark*, 42 Cdo was selected for sea service in the latter and found itself on active service in Kuwait and, later, rescuing European hostages during the Brunei revolt. Aden was the unit's next operational area, but it was disbanded from its Far Eastern role in 1971. Since then, Northern Ireland has been the scene of a number of deployments, but in 1978 the unit was earmarked for mountain and arctic warfare. The troops are now all ski qualified and the unit's conventional role is now supporting NATO's Northern Flank, although it deployed to the South Atlantic in 1982 and fought successfully on Mounts Kent and Harriet, being also involved in the liberation of South Georgia and Southern Thule.

In 1971, a year of great change in the Royal Marines as Britain pulled away from its Far Eastern role, 45 Commando Group was formed at Condor Base, the former Royal Naval Air Station near Arbroath in Scotland. This Group is assigned to NATO and was the United Kingdom's first Mountain and Arctic Warfare Unit; it spends several months every year operating in northern Norway, the NATO Northern Flank. 'Four Five' Commando actually dates back to 1943, and has always recruited from Scotland and the north of England.

## MOUNTAIN AND ARCTIC WARFARE

The modern Royal Marine is closely associated with the tough training carried out annually since 1970 in northern Norway when

*Mountain & Arctic Warfare commandos collect their kit after being flown into a remote location by Sea King HC 4 helicopter. Note that the personal weapon being used is the new SA 80 (Patrick Allen).*

the first Marines from 45 Commando arrived on the NATO Northern Flank. Marines trained in Norway are now expert skiers, mountain and ice climbers and icefield trekkers, and are skilled at all aspects of living out of doors in the Arctic. Today, some 3,000 RM Commandos can ski well and several hundred speak good colloquial Norwegian.

Norway is now the major commitment of the Corps, and its way of warfare will involve operations in both summer heat and the winter snows. Mountain and Arctic Warfare training has been developed into an art and a science, with most men capable of building good snow-holes, climbing rock-faces and moving safely across areas in freezing temperatures. Not only does a Marine have to know about living and surviving against the elements, he must also be able to fight.

## OIL PLATFORM SECURITY

With the increased threat of terrorism against British and allied North Sea oil platforms, the Royal Marines formed Comacchio Company (now Comacchio Group) in 1980 to protect the offshore installations. Commandos can be moved to the rigs by various means, including helicopter, canoe, landing craft and parachute.

Much of the work of this Arbroath-based unit is classified to maintain the defence against terrorism, but frequent exercises are held to ensure that there is an effective deterrent against attack.

## ABOARD SHIP

Royal Marines have always served aboard Her Majesty's ships and in 1978 the Ministry of Defence implemented an increase in small ship detachments for frigates and destroyers. These detachments were to provide the nucleus of naval landing parties but also to undertake regular 'housekeeping' duties aboard ship, including some bridge watchkeeping.

## SMALL CRAFT

Besides the men aboard Royal Naval warships, there are a number of small craft closely associated with the Royal Marines, especially landing craft. The Corps began its association with these military craft in 1943 and controlled the assault elements of amphibious landings. Today, however, it is not considered standard operational

*Oil installation protection in the North Sea is carried out by Comacchio Group based at Arbroath and using a variety of methods to protect and if necessary liberate oil platforms.*

practice to deploy troops, including Marines, across a beach-head under hostile fire, but rather to land them first to deter aggression.

Nevertheless, there is still a need and a role for the landing craft and other assault equipment, especially in the Northern Flank defence task. During the 1980s, the Royal Marines have experi-

**Above** *Amphibious operations include the use of Landing Craft Utility (LCUs) either from an Assault Ship or acting independently. Aerial support is provided by helicopters, such as this Gazelle AH 1 from 3 Cdo Bde Air Sqn RM (Patrick Allen).*

**Below** *Raiding craft, such as the Dell Quay Rigid Raider, are used for carrying up to nine troops behind enemy lines, often at night, to raid enemy positions. This boat belongs to 1 Raiding Sqn RM and was photographed in Norway (Commando Forces News Team).*

mented with the use of specially-equipped landing craft to operate all year round in Arctic Norway and to be capable of making the crossing from Scotland under their own power. Aboard the Assault Ships *Fearless* and *Intrepid* there are four utility landing craft and four smaller craft for personnel and small vehicles. To control these and to guide the forces ashore, each ship has an Assault Squadron.

Closely associated with the Assault Squadrons are the raiding craft used by small groups of men to penetrate enemy beaches; these are either rigid raiders or inflatable Gemini craft operated from the casings of submarines. There is a raiding squadron in Hong Kong which was originally formed to support the local forces and civilian police in the apprehension of fast boats bringing in illegal immigrants from the People's Republic of China.

The Special Boat Squadron, another small craft unit, is often called the Royal Marines' equivalent of the British Army's Special Air Service, but the SBS is not such an elitist organization and it does not have a cadre of long-serving personnel. It relies, instead, on the professional ability of every Royal Marine — it claims that it can do everything expected of the SAS 'and walk on water'!

## COMMANDO BRIGADE AIR SQUADRON

Formed in 1968 at Dieppe Barracks, Singapore, the 3rd Commando Brigade Air Squadron Royal Marines (3 Cdo Bde Air Sqn RM) is better known in the Corps as the BAS (pronounced 'bass'). The original equipment was the Westland-Agusta-built version of the American Bell 47 Sioux battlefield observation and liaison helicopter which were supplemented by Westland Scout before the unit returned to the United Kingdom in 1971.

Although definitely part of the Royal Navy, the Royal Marines draw much of their equipment from the British Army and the BAS is no exception, its equipment and training basically mirroring that of the Army Air Corps. The squadron also maintains close links with the Fleet Air Arm, using its survival equipment and aircraft handlers.

In 1975, the Sioux was replaced by the Gazelle in the forward observation role and later, in 1983, the Scout was replaced by the TOW anti-missile armed Lynx. This gives the Squadron some of the best equipment available in the world.

Some of the Squadron's flights had completed 18 operational tours in Northern Ireland before being sent to the Falkland Islands in 1982 where they supported the ground forces with tremendous

The primary liaison and observation helicopter of the Royal
Marines is the Westland-built
Aerospatiale Gazelle AH 1,
recovering aboard Sir Geraint's
small flight deck. Note the letters
RM marked on the underside,
the homing aerials and the Dop-
pler tactical navigation system
(Patrick Allen).

success. This squadron alone was awarded one OBE, two BEMs,
one MC, two DFCs, a DFM, nine Mentions in Despatches and four
Queen's Commendations for Valuable Service in the Air.

Each year, flights are deployed with the Commando forces to
Norway (after re-familiarization with mountainous conditions in
the French Pyrenees), Denmark and Northern Ireland. On a less
regular basis, helicopters from the BAS have operated in Canada,
the United States, the West Indies, Asia, the Far East, Australia and
parts of East and West Africa.

Today, the Squadron provides reconnaissance and anti-tank
helicopter support to units of the Commando Forces.

## HEADQUARTERS AND SIGNALS SQUADRON

In 1971, the Royal Marines formed a special headquarters and
signals squadron to provide the commander with appropriate
facilities to control the Commando Brigade in peace and war. The

squadron is split into a number of troops: Command, Administrative, Communications, Motor Transport, Police, Tactical Air Control and Air Defence.

## COMMANDO LOGISTIC REGIMENT

The formation of this Royal Marines unit began in July 1971 as the support element of 3 Commando Brigade, and now uses the talents of various Royal Marines and British Army units to provide medical, transport, ordnance and workshop support for Commando Forces in the United Kingdom and around the world.

To administer the regiment in its diverse roles there are five squadrons, and these were tested during the Falklands campaign when more than half the Regiment's personnel were deployed to the South Atlantic, staying on after the cessation of hostilities to clean up and recover *matériel* to the UK. During the conflict, the Regiment moved some 9,000 tons of stores, treated more than 1,000 casualties and operated helicopter landing sites for the beachhead forces.

## FIRE SUPPORT

Providing the basically infantry Royal Marines Commandos with artillery is a special Commando-trained regiment of the Royal Artillery which was raised in 1961 and received Commando training in 1962. Later that same year, the Regiment was operational in Brunei, being the first unit to use the 105mm Pak howitzer in anger.

To support the commitments of today's Royal Marines, 29 Cdo Regt Royal Artillery is made up of three gun batteries, a command forward observation battery, a Territorial Army battery and a Headquarters unit.

Supporting 40 Cdo is 8 (Alma) Battery, 42 Cdo is supported by 79 (Kirkee) Battery and 45 Cdo by 7 (Spinx) battery, each with six 105mm light guns, while the Commando Forward Observation Battery is 148 (Meiktila) Battery.

Based at Plymouth, 59 Independent Commando Squadron Royal Engineers is the other British Army Commando-trained unit to support 3 Commando Brigade Royal Marines. For most of this century there has been a close relationship between the Royal Engineers and the Royal Marines, but the present form of the Squadron was only completed in 1971, after the withdrawal from

*Artillery support for the Royal Marines is provided by the 105 mm Light Guns of 29 Cdo Regt Royal Artillery who are commando-trained members of the British Army, fully integrated within the Commando Forces.*

East of Suez. The Squadron is responsible for all engineer work within the brigade area, including mine laying, mine clearance, route maintenance, bridging, rafting, water supplies and snow clearance. During the Falklands conflict, the Squadron provided engineer support to all Commando units.

# RNR – THE VITAL RESERVE

By the early 1990s, some 7,800 men and women will have volunteered and been accepted as members of the Royal Naval Reserve, a force which trains in its spare time for a variety of sea, air and shore-based tasks in support of the regular Royal Navy and the defence of the Western Alliance. Training is highly professional and is now fully integrated with the Royal Navy.

In certain areas, such as naval control of shipping (organizing and controlling the vital convoys of merchant ships world-wide in wartime) and deep-water mines countermeasures, the use of the RNR is essential to a balanced naval force.

The RNR's history goes back to the decision to train a reserve of merchant seamen and later, with the perceived threat from the Imperial German Navy, the decision was made to form a volunteer force of civilians with an interest in the sea. Initially the Royal Naval Reserve and the Royal Naval Volunteer Reserves were men-only organizations but by the Second World War it was obvious that women had an equally important role to play, although the Women's Royal Naval Volunteer Reserve was not founded until 1951. In 1958, the Admiralty decided to streamline the reserve forces and created by amalgamation the Royal Naval Reserve (men) and the Women's Royal Naval Reserve (women) to cover all the previous lists.

In the 1980s, the RNR is commanded by Commander-in-Chief Naval Home Command through the Reserves Division which includes the University Royal Naval Units, Naval Cadet Forces and the Royal Navy-sponsored Sea Scout Groups. CINCNAVHOME's staff is responsible for policy, shore training, pay, recruitment, publicity and personnel administration through the office of the Chief Staff Officer (Reserves), but direct command and administration of the units in the United Kingdom, Gibraltar and Hong Kong has been passed to the relevant Area Flag Officers.

The RNR mans the 'River' Class minesweepers of the 10th Mines Countermeasures Squadron; these ships come under the operational control of Commander-in-Chief Fleet through the Commodore Minor War Vessels and the Senior Officer 10th MCM Squadron who also controls sea training. In addition to this primary

*10th Mines Countermeasures Squadron, the Royal Naval Reserve manned unit, is now fully re-equipped with the 'River' Class coastal minesweeper and expects to supplement these with the single-role 'Sandown' Class minehunter by 1990. Blackwater is seen off Gibraltar (RN).*

role, the RNR now trains in peacetime for many wartime tasks; these include manning ships taken up from trade (for mines countermeasures) and patrol craft for the defence of ports and anchorages, providing logistical support liaison officers for merchant ships, forward engineering support, naval control of shipping, manning maritime, port and communications headquarters, back up for front-line aircrew, intelligence, security and press liaison, Fleet mail, casualty evacuation and mobile surgical support of the Commando forces, augmentation of Fleet clearance diving teams and the manning of degaussing ranges.

The Royal Naval Reserve goes to sea from Sea Training Centres in Sea Tenders which are either the 'River' Class MCMVs, which have replaced the faithful 'Ton' Class minesweepers and minehunters, or the 'Tracker' Class patrol vessels. Sea Training Centres are found around the British coast and at Belfast (where the headquarters is established in a former First World War light cruiser, *Caroline*, moored alongside). Ashore, the RNR makes use of six Headquarters Units and a dozen Communications Training Centres.

The Headquarters Reserve was formed in 1956 to provide trained ratings to support the Maritime Headquarters in Scotland, London and Plymouth with locally-based volunteers. Today, the modern Royal Naval Reserve has found considerable value in the HQ personnel training and has extended the system to Gibraltar, Greenock and Chatham.

Similarly based at onshore centres, the RNR Communications network was originally formed in 1932 and now trains communications officers and ratings to man ships, maritime headquarters, communications centres and Port Headquarters.

For the British Universities at Aberdeen, Glasgow/Strathclyde, Liverpool, London and Southampton, there are special Royal Naval units (URNUs) where undergraduates can enrol as honorary Midshipmen RNR, especially if they are considering a full-time

*Royal Naval Reserve personnel regularly train at sea and still use the ancient mariner arts of navigation by sun and stars to back up the ships' modern technology. This officer wears the insignia of a Lieutenant RNR.*

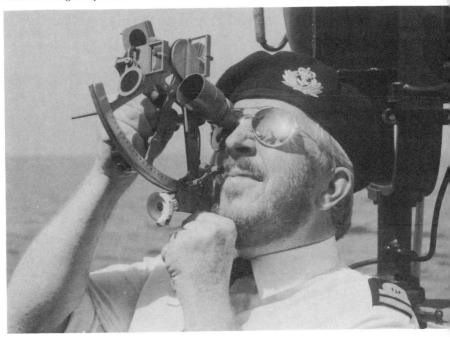

career or part-time service in the Royal Navy. For those attending other Universities, there are opportunities at the local Sea Training Centres, provided that the student is within a reasonable travelling distance. The URNUs have access to training craft. Naval Control of Shipping units are to be found in the Channel Islands, Hong Kong, Hull, Pembroke Docks, Norwich and Aberdeen, while across the rest of the United Kingdom there are some 150 Combined Cadet Forces, 400 Sea Cadet Corps units and over 100 other recognized young people's units.

Every year, apart from the regular training nights, the RNR and WRNR are involved in major exercises, including naval control of shipping and convoy courses, as well as being away at sea on naval exercises. In 1986, mines countermeasures vessels of 10th MCM Squadron were involved in Exercise Rockhaul, off Gibraltar, which included working with Spanish naval units and other NATO forces.

Male ratings who leave the Royal Navy 'honourably' before completing a pensionable engagement are required to serve three years in the Royal Fleet Reserve. At the end of 1986 there were some 4,300 such men, who form a valuable part of the RN's mobilization plan for any future conflict. In 1986, annual reporting for these ratings was introduced, replacing the rather more tenuous contact practised before. The new system will allow all RFR ratings to register and collect a new improved bounty, and the eventual aim is to give each man a war job to which he can report in the event of hostilities.

Finally, the specialist press relations, medical, aircrew, diving and similar branches of the Royal Naval Reserve are also expanding to cope with the increased needs of the defence of the United Kingdom and the NATO Alliance.

# THE ROYAL FLEET AUXILIARY

Since the days of the Elizabethan sailing ships, the Royal Navy has been supported at sea by merchant ships which have formed, since the Napoleonic Wars, the professional auxiliary body, known today as the Royal Fleet Auxiliary Service. The RFA remains merchant-flagged with a professional cadre of officers and seamen who proudly boast the Service's motto 'Ready for Anything' — or more usually 'RN sails courtesy RFA'.

The RFA is managed by the Director of Supplies and Transport (Ships & Fuel), being one of five directorates which eventually report to the Chief of Naval Support, an Admiralty Board member. RFA ships are not just confined to fuel carriers, and are today highly specialized as the Royal Navy's role develops to counter possible threats around the world.

*RFA integration with the Royal Navy is almost total. Here two junior radio officers are undergoing communications systems training at Collingwood, the RN shore establishment near Gosport (RN).*

On any one day, RFAs will be supporting RN warships wherever they may be, including the Falkland Islands patrol, the Arabian Sea patrol, the Norwegian Sea, the Mediterranean and the Western Atlantic naval ranges where warships regularly go for live firing and other trials. The most common operation between RFA and warship is replenishment at sea, which calls for a high degree of seamanship. This is a regular occurrence, happening perhaps as often as every three days during a warship deployment. During the Falklands conflict, this was the only way of replenishing warships which eventually operated out of port for almost three months.

The demands of the modern warship have grown since the Fleet Trains of the Second World War, especially so since the development of small ship naval aviation. To cater for the demands of operational service, the RFA is now developing a range of 'one-stop' ships which will enable a single replenishment at sea of fuel, liquids, solid and specialist stores, a tricky manoeuvre for both RFA and warship.

RAS(L) — replenishment at sea (liquids) — includes the transfer of fuel oil, and one, two or even more ships can be replenished simultaneously, while allowing manoeuvre room so that anti-submarine precautions can be observed. This also applies, but in a more limited way, to RAS(S) — replenishment at sea (solids) — which utilizes the RFA's jackstay rigs. Since most RFAs, as well as the ship to be replenished will usually operate helicopters, there is the third possibility that an RAS will be by vertrep (vertical replenishment) using the helicopter's underslung load capability. This is especially useful for weapons and urgent stores and also means that a further ship can be replenished whilst others are

**Left** *The move towards 'one-stop' ships began with the commissioning of the 'Fort' Class replenishment and stores ships. This is* Fort Austin *during a RAS (S) using a Sea King HAS 5; four such helicopters can be carried in these ships and operated for ASW and other tasks* (RN/LA Photo T. Harding).

**Below** *Replenishment at sea requires skill and expertise found in very few navies, but as warships need to replenish regularly in all weathers and conditions, it is an exercise practiced regularly. This is the tanker* Brambleleaf *during a RAS (L).*

carrying out side-by-side replenishment while under way.

In the late 1980s, the Royal Fleet Auxiliary Service operates a number of different types of ships to fulfil the necessary roles, especially for NATO exercises. Amongst the largest ships under Ministry of Defence control are the Large Fleet Tankers of the 'Ol' Class, *Olwen, Olna* and *Olmeda.* These vessels displace some 36,000 tons (including over 24,250 tons of oil) and can operate as many as four Sea King helicopters for vertrep or as a platform for Fleet anti-submarine operations. A graceful design of tanker is the *Tidespring,* last of the 'Tide' Class which first entered service in the 1960s for the replenishment of aircraft carriers and other large warships. It

*Two 'Rover' Class escort tankers at sea off the Isle of Wight during an exercise. Most Royal Fleet Auxiliary ships have flight decks to assist with the transfer of netted loads and some provide platforms for helicopter operations as a supplement to the warships.*

displaces 27,400 tons and can carry 18,860 tons of oil and some other stores. Again, *Tidespring* can operate helicopters as required.

For the replenishment of frigates and destroyers, and possessing the same performance and endurance, the 'Rover' Class have been which they were specially designed. Each of the five ships in service is capable of providing 6,600 tons of furnace fuel oil, diesel, aviation spirit, lubricating oil, fresh water and some dry cargos. Although the ships do not have helicopter hangarage, they all possess a flight deck (which has been cleared for Sea Harrier jet operations) and from which warship helicopters can be used for vertrep.

Supporting the 'Ol', 'Tide' and 'Rover' Classes are the 'Leaf' Class tankers, used to top up the other refuellers. They also have a special but limited RAS capability, which is fitted as and when the vessels are chartered by the Ministry of Defence in London. Like all RFAs and warships, they are capable of light jackstay transfers of mail, personnel and high-value items.

Designed for a more general role is the 'Fort' Class of two fast

Fleet Replenishment Ships which were designed to provide an under-way top-up service of ammunition, food and other dry cargo stores. Aboard the 'Forts' the stores are on pallets for greater efficiency in handling. Besides the more usual stores role, this class has also been a pioneer in the use of embarked anti-submarine helicopters and was designed to carry the Sea King. Right aft there is a flight deck and hangar, and the hangar roof itself is another flight deck where helicopters can be re-armed and refuelled, allowing multiple helicopter operations. One Admiral has described the use of the 'Fort' Class RFAs in an exercise as like having another aircraft carrier deck available for sustained ASW operations.

Longer serving than the 'Forts' are *Regent* and *Resource* which were ordered in the early 1960s to escort the remaining conventional fixed-wing aircraft carriers and provide top-up of ammunition and some air stores. The two 'Regents' can supply ammunition, explosives, food, naval stores and aircraft spares either by jackstay transfer or using the embarked Wessex HU 5 helicopter. The ships have a full displacement of nearly 23,000 tons.

There cannot be many who do not remember the courageous rescue operation by Fleet Air Arm helicopters at Bluff Cove in 1982 when the Landing Ships *Sir Galahad* and *Sir Tristram* were bombed and badly damaged by Argentine aircraft during an operation to move a reinforced battalion of the Welsh Guards closer to Port Stanley. It is not widely known, however, that these ships, known as LSLs — Landing Ships Logistic — were part of a class of five RFAs built during the mid-1960s. All five were present in the South Atlantic, carrying the helicopters of the Commando Brigade Air Squadron Royal Marines and other equipment.

So vital are the LSLs to British reinforcement plans for Europe, especially Norway, that two Ro-Ro ferries, *Sir Caradoc* and *Sir Lamorak*, were hired for replacements until *Sir Tristram* was repaired and the new *Sir Galahad* built. The latter was launched in December 1986 and will join the Service in 1988, having been built with a large number of refinements born of the South Atlantic experience.

Also as a result of the Falklands, there have been other changes in the RFA, including the provision of defensive systems for RFAs which could lead to re-definition of the ships as warships during the next few years. Three new types will also enter service by 1990, one as a direct result of the need to keep warships in the South Atlantic.

*Diligence*, the former North Sea multi-purpose repair and re-supply ship *Stena Inspector*, was purchased by the Ministry of

**Above** Sir Percival is one of six Landing Ships Logistic which are manned by the Royal Fleet Auxiliary Service and support the needs of the Royal Navy and Marines, as well as the British Army. All six were operational in the Falklands Islands (Robin Walker).

**Below** Specialist depot and forward repair ship Diligence is based in San Carlos water in the Falklands to assist warships on guard duty. In this picture, a Sikorsky S-61N on contract from Bristow Helicopters is landing on the flight deck, whilst the 'Leander' Class frigate Penelope is moored alongside (Falklands Photo Section).

Defence for the RFA in October 1983 and is now stationed in San Carlos Water to act as a base for the visiting warships, including nuclear-powered submarines, and she is capable of accepting Chinook-size medium-lift helicopters. Aboard there is a full array of accommodation, workshops, stores and other necessities for a warship's assisted maintenance. In August 1987 she was deployed to the Gulf.

Also given impetus by the campaign were the orders for the first 'One-stop AOR' from Harland & Wolff, to be called *Fort Victoria*, and the new Aviation Training Ship *Argus*, both important for the RFA. *Fort Victoria* is a 31,500-tonne vessel capable of 18 knots and armed with Sea Wolf point-defence missiles and a full array of self-defence countermeasure launchers. Command and control of the ship is possible through the use of a Ferranti Computer system, making her the most sophisticated replenishment ship in Europe. Replacing the faithful *Engadine*, on which most naval pilots have deck qualified, the new Aviation Training Ship is herself almost akin to an aircraft carrier. She is designed to carry six Sea Kings with an aviation complement of 42 officers and 95 ratings, or be capable of taking 12 Sea Harrier fighters to any theatre in the world, with the

*Nearing completion in the Belfast yard of Harland & Wolff is the aviation training ship Argus which replaced Engadine in late 1987. The ship uses merchant ship construction, retaining many of the features of a container ship (Harland & Wolff).*

capability of flying off at the end of the voyage. *Argus* (formerly known as *Contender Bezant*) has a larger hangar than the 'Invincible' Class CVSs and will be based at Portland when she comes into fully operational service.

There are also a number of proposals for an Aviation Support Ship being considered by the Admiralty. This ship is required to replace *Hermes*, the light aircraft carrier paid off in 1983 and later sold to India. The new LPH (Landing Platform Helicopter) would be RFA-manned but be capable of carrying 800 men in a reinforced Royal Marines Commando, together with twelve Sea King HC 4 or similar helicopters.

Although in naval operational terms there can never be enough Royal Fleet Auxiliaries in service, the modern RFA is efficient and well run, and has a special place in the annals of the Royal Navy.

# WOMEN IN THE ROYAL NAVY

Unlike many of Europe's maritime forces, the Women's Royal Naval Service and the Women's Royal Naval Reserve are separate organizations under the umbrella of the Royal Navy. Although they are not integrated and only a few go to sea, and then never to permanent combat postings, women are vital to the everyday running of the modern Royal Navy.

During the First World War, women were encouraged to undertake clerical and support jobs to allow more men to fight, but it was not until the Second World War that the WRNS was formed. The 'Wrens' have their own independent rank and rating structure, from the Director, who holds the rank of Commandant (equivalent to a Commodore Royal Navy), down to Ordinary Wren. Although subject to the Naval Discipline Act, WRNS personnel have specific and important exemptions.

Ashore, Wrens are found in almost every part of the Royal Navy

Commandant WRNS *Britain's most senior woman sailor is the Commandant of the Women's Royal Naval Service, the equivalent of a Commodore. Since February 1986, the post has been held by Commandant M. H. Fletcher ADC WRNS who joined the Service in 1953. Her appointments have included secretarial duties on the staff of Flag Officer Reserve Aircraft, Commander-in-Chief Allied Mediterranean and the Defence Intelligence Staff. Miss Fletcher passed out of the National Defence College, Latimer, Buckinghamshire. More recently, before promotion to Commandant and appointment as the Director WRNS, Miss Fletcher was the first WRNS officer to serve as Assistant Director of International and Bilateral Relations.*

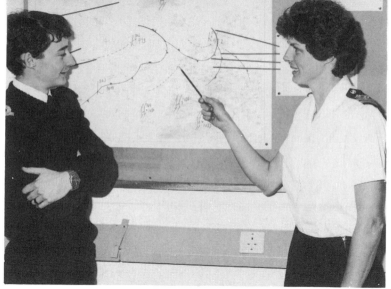

Second Officer WRNS Second Officers WRNS hold an equivalent rank to Lieutenants RN and carry out similar appointments. Nikki Hamp joined the WRNS in September 1979 from Aberystwyth University and one of her jobs was analysing surface gunnery exercises, on the staff of Captain Weapon Trials. In January 1981 she was accepted for officer training at BRNC Dartmouth and commissioned with rank of Third Officer in March 1981, joining 737 Naval Air Squadron as an administrator. She studied Meteorology in 1983 and was posted to Culdrose as a watch-keeping Weather Forecaster and as Divisional Officer to Meteorological Wrens at the naval air station. Nikki Hamp intends to leave the Service in March 1989 at the end of an eight year's Short Career Commission. She is married to a Lieutenant (Observer) in the Fleet Air Arm (RN/Culdrose).

Chief Wren CWREN Robson joined the WRNS in 1972 after attending an Outward Bound Course while working as a civilian for the Ministry of Defence. Between 1972 and 1973 she qualified as a Dental Surgery Assistant, then as Education Assistant. Various appointments followed including duty in Mauritius, Scotland and Cornwall. Her latest posting is to Culdrose and she is married to a Chief Petty Officer in the Fleet Air Arm (RN/Culdrose).

*Both men and women attend courses at Britannia Royal Naval College, Dartmouth, where they learn all the skills to become naval officers. At the end of term, Lord High Admiral's Division take place in the presence of the Queen, who is the Lord High Admiral (RN).*

and are playing important roles in naval aviation, the submarine flotilla and specialist analysis and administrative jobs. Just as the Royal Navy mirrors British society, so the role of women in naval uniform changes, including today a greater emphasis on equal opportunities to undertake specialist work.

As with their male colleagues, new entry Wrens undertake their initial training at *Raleigh* near Plymouth, and officers are trained at the Britannia Royal Naval College, Dartmouth. A large number enter the Air Branch as aircraft handlers or for meteorology, while others become air engineering mechanics; some are more 'domestic' in their sub-specializations, becoming dental hygienists, surgery assistants, writers and educationalists.

One of the more interesting specializations now available is that of Wren Weapon Analyst, serving at naval air stations, weapon ranges and in various units where guided and unguided weapons are tested. Her job may also require brief periods at sea to assess in real conditions the programmes to which she is assigned, including the development of new missiles.

## NAVAL NURSES

The senior women's service for the Royal Navy is Queen Alexandra's Royal Naval Nursing Service, an important part of the Royal Naval Medical Service, the branch primarily responsible for the health and

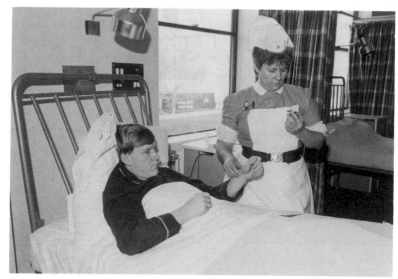

*The Queen Alexandra's Royal Naval Nursing Service provides 'tender loving care' for servicemen ill or injured. This is part of the modern Sick Bay facilities at the main Plymouth area establishment and barracks, Drake (RN/Drake).*

fitness of the Royal Navy, Royal Marines, Women's Royal Naval Service and certain Ministry of Defence civil servants. The service began life in 1902, although specialist naval nursing dates back to the Crimea, 50 years before. During the Second World War, there were 1,200 QARNNS, and they now serve in the major hospital complexes at Haslar (Portsmouth), Stonehouse (Plymouth) and Gibraltar. Until 1982, entry into the QARNNS was restricted to women, but since then men have been welcomed.

Nurses are selected from applicants with or without previous nursing experience but who have a good educational background and a vocation for nursing. They are trained at Haslar and at the National Health Service hospital at Cosham.

Nursing Officers are selected from Registered General Nurse applicants for training at Haslar and Stonehouse prior to their appointment as Nursing Officer (equivalent to a Third Officer WRNS) or Senior Nursing Officer. Advancement is on selection, seniority and post-qualification experience to Matron-in-Chief — this a job title rather than a promotion when, on rotation, the QARNNS provide the Director of Defence Nursing Services.

QARNNS do not serve at sea except, as in the Falklands conflict, on hospital ships taken up from trade. Overseas billets include

Matron-in-Chief QARNNS Britain's most senior naval nurse, the Matron-in-Chief, is Eileen Northway who qualified as a State Registered Nurse in 1952 and joined the Queen Alexandra's Royal Naval Nursing Service in 1956 with the rank of Senior Nursing officer. In the 1960s, Miss Northway was posted to Malta and Hong Kong, and later to the Royal Marines at Deal. With promotion to the rank of Matron in 1978, she was appointed to Royal Naval Hospital Haslar as the Matron, later to the staff of Surgeon Rear Admiral (Naval Hospitals) in the rank of Principal Matron (now styled Principal Nursing Officer). Before being appointed as Matron-in-Chief in June 1986, Miss Northway was the Deputy. On rotation the Matron-in-Chief QARNNS is also Director of Defence Nursing Services (DPR(N)).

Family Clinics in Hong Kong and Naples, while in the UK, besides the Royal Naval Hospitals, you will find QARNNS in establishment sick bays.

## CORRESPONDING RANKS

| Royal Navy | Women's Royal Naval Service | QARNNS |
|---|---|---|
| Admiral of the Fleet | – | – |
| Admiral | – | – |
| Vice Admiral | – | – |
| Rear Admiral | Chief Commandant | – |
| Commodore | Commandant | Matron-in-Chief |
| Captain | Superintendent | Principal Nursing Officer |
| Commander | Chief Officer | Chief Nursing Officer |
| Lt Commander | First Officer | Superintending Nursing Officer |
| Lieutenant | Second Officer | Senior Nursing Officer |
| Sub Lieutenant | Third Officer | Nursing Officer |
| | | |
| Warrant Officer | Warrant Officer (Wren) | Warrant Officer (RGN) |
| Chief Petty Officer | Chief Wren | Chief Petty Officer |
| Petty Officer | Petty Officer Wren | Petty Officer Nurse |
| Leading Rate | Leading Wren | Leading Nurse |
| Able Rate | Wren (Able) | Student Nurse |
| Ordinary Rate | Wren (Ordinary) | Probationary Student Nurse |

# INDEX

Page numbers in italics indicate photographs.